ON THE HUNT

ON THE HUNT

HOW TO WAKE UP WASHINGTON
AND WIN THE WAR ON TERROR

COLONEL DAVID HUNT
(U.S. ARMY, RET.)

CROWN
FORUM
NEW YORK

Published in the United States by Crown Forum, an imprint of the
Crown Publishing Group, a division of Random House, Inc., New York.
www.crownpublishing.com

Crown Forum and the Crown Forum colophon are trademarks of
Random House, Inc.

Library of Congress Cataloging-in-Publication Data
Hunt, David, Colonel.
On the Hunt : how to wake up Washington and win the war on terror /
David Hunt. —1st ed.
p. cm.
Includes bibliographical references.
1. War on Terrorism, 2001–   2. Iraq War, 2003–   3. Terrorism—
Government policy—United States.   4. National security—United
States.   5. United States—Military policy.   I. Title.
HV6432.H84 2007
363.325'15610973—dc22
2006039187

978-0-307-34759-6

Printed in the United States of America

Design by Leonard Henderson

10 9 8 7 6 5 4 3 2 1

First Edition

For those who are serving in our great military today, and for those who served in wars past—men like my brother Joey, who died in Quang Tri in 1968, and my dad, who served in the Pacific during World War II from Bougainville through Iwo Jima.

They are the bravest men I ever knew. Those in the fight now honor them and us.

CONTENTS

ON THE HUNT

CHAPTER 1

RIGHT IN FRONT OF US

Riding at thirty-five miles an hour on a behemoth that can kill from more than two miles away, wind and sand in your face, diesel fumes in your nose, men yelling in your ear on a radio, bad guys dying on the side of the road, you are exhausted—you haven't slept in thirty-six hours, and when you do sleep, it will be in a hole you dig—but absolutely elated, knowing you and your brave men are finally doing what you have been trained to do for so many years.

All this was going through Colonel Dave Perkins's mind as he led his brigade of tanks and mechanized infantry across the Iraqi desert in March 2003. His soldiers were performing perfectly. His unit was ahead of the plan. He was a warrior god doing what he does best.

Perkins got his 5,000-man unit to a spot outside of Baghdad where his superiors wanted him to stop and wait. They wanted him to be a "good colonel" and ask permission before he entered the capital. He could have sat back, waited for permission, and spent days as a sitting duck while his superiors had three meetings, two briefings, and an ass-chewing before determining whether Saddam Hussein had set a trap inside Baghdad. Instead, Colonel Perkins took a risk: he made a dash for

1

Baghdad. He called it a "Thunder Run" because of the speed, power, and noise of that many tanks running down the road.

It was an audacious, tactically risky move. And it was goddamned brilliant. Perkins's brave decision shortened the war and saved his guys. Colonel Dave Perkins is exactly the type of leader that makes our military great; we need more like him.

A few miles to the south of this great guy and his great men, a different story was unfolding.

Task Force Tarawa was a 1,000-man Marine unit moving up the right side of Iraq. Intel told them that the town they were about to hit, Nasiriya, was full of Shiites and very friendly to us. The operation was going to be a piece of cake. But the Marines didn't find friendly crowds in Nasiriya; they found a fight, a fight so bad that at several points they thought they might lose—not a thing any Marine contemplates well. An Army maintenance company had already come under attack there, and several soldiers, including the now famous Private Jessica Lynch, were missing inside the city. Bad maps, bad communications, and "friendly" civilians who took up arms alongside the Sunni Saddam Fedayeen troops and some desperate foreign jihadis all conspired to give us a wake-up call that the Iraq war was not as it had been advertised.[1]

Unfortunately, we did not hear it.

These two battles demonstrate the underlying systematic problems we are having fighting the Global War on Terror. After we took Baghdad, we paraded around using the swift capture as an example of our might. We touted our win in Baghdad like the government touts the fact that we have not been attacked on American soil since 9/11: as if that demonstrates victory. It does not.

The guys who took Baghdad did a great job, but this one instance did not a winning strategy make, especially when at the same time there was also Nasiriya. What did we do after the Nasiriya battle? We did nothing. We ignored it. We ignored the fact that the Marines almost lost the battle like we would later ignore the insurgency, like we would ignore terrorist attacks that happened all over the world as if they didn't have anything to do with us. We didn't look at Nasiriya and figure out what went wrong. We didn't study it and learn how to prevent that kind of thing from happening in the future. We hid our heads in the sand and missed the lessons that we should have learned. The result of this is the chaos in Iraq and the terrorists who are winning in such places as Lebanon and Palestine. We ignore these lessons at our own peril.

In all wars, and specifically the wars we are fighting now, how well we do is important, but how badly we do is more important—not only because our guys get killed and maimed and our country suffers but also because hidden within the losses and mistakes are the keys to winning the next battle and ultimately the war.

In order to win the War on Terror we need to look at things as they truly happen and not as we wish them to be. We covered our eyes after Nasiriya when it should have alerted us to all the things that were going to go wrong—bad intelligence, bad communications, bad gear, bad leadership, bad training, ill-prepared soldiers, and flawed rules of engagement.

This book takes a hard look at the stuff that has gone wrong—on the battlefields abroad and right here at home—in the hopes that we will be able to take from them the things we need to know to prevent the next attack.

WHERE WE ARE NOW

People who recognize me from my appearances on the Fox News Channel often come up to me and ask, "Colonel, where are we in the War on Terror?" I'm not a big fan of sugarcoating or bullshitting, so let me tell you, right here at the beginning, that I won't be putting a happy face on this war. I can't. Our brave soldiers, Marines, and Special Forces are doing amazing things for us, and many of them are giving their lives to protect us. We long to believe that the incredible things they're doing are bringing us close to victory in this war. Hell, I'd love to be able to tell you that we're winning. But I can't do that. The truth is, the War on Terror is not going well, not well at all. We've known from the beginning of this war that we're engaged in a monumental struggle for our very survival, one that will take not months or years to win but decades. The way we've been fighting, however, doesn't make it seem like we get that. Not at all.

It's not just Iraq. We've got huge problems in Afghanistan. The rest of the Middle East is screwed up. We've badly mishandled Iran and North Korea. (Can you say "Axis of Evil"?)

In 2005, I wrote a book called *They Just Don't Get It* because I was scared and pissed off. I knew we were making mistakes in the War on Terror and I tried to show how we could win the war and protect ourselves better. Our leaders needed to make some big changes, and fast.

Sadly, though, they *still* don't get it.

Don't get me wrong—we've done some great things in the War on Terror. Anyone who denies our successes is a fool or, worse, trying to score political points. Just look at some of our achievements:

- Our armed forces have heroically taken the fight to the terrorists in back alleys and caves around the world. They fight in the frigid cold and lung-destroying altitudes of Afghanistan, and in 125-degree, hot-enough-to-fry-an-egg-on-your-helmet heat in Iraq.
- We've given other countries a chance at this thing we call freedom. In Afghanistan more than 12.5 million people, including 6 million women, have registered to vote. Iraq has held free elections for the first time in history.
- We have inoculated the children of Iraq and rebuilt, or built from scratch, thousands of schools, hospitals, roads, and bridges.
- Oh, yeah, and we kicked Saddam Hussein's ass. Don't think that matters? Tell that to the families of the victims of terrorists Saddam supported—the Palestinian suicide bombers he funded over the years, or terrorist honchos like Abu Abbas and Abu Nidal, for whom the Iraqi dictator provided safe haven.
- Even our intelligence agencies—which I've been very critical of over the years—have done some good things. The bottom line is that there hasn't been another major terrorist attack in the United

States since 9/11. That's good, for sure. Our intelligence community has stopped some other bad things from happening and arrested some very bad people. We've foiled at least three different al-Qaeda hijacking plots—one targeting London, another focusing on the U.S. consulate in Pakistan, and a third aimed at the United States, Britain, Italy, and Australia.[2] And this is just the stuff we know about.

All this is important. We can and should be proud of our list of accomplishments. But the list should be much longer and much stronger. And in particular, it should include a lot more things that directly affect the enemy—like, say, killing the terrorists' leaders.

A lot of this is common sense, whether some of our military and political leaders want to admit it or not. When a forty-year-old baseball player has arms, neck, and a chest bigger than Hercules', it's common sense to think he might be taking something stronger than vitamins. It's the same thing with the War on Terror. When, five years into the War on Terror, Osama bin Laden can go on television time and time again and his buddy Ayman al-Zawahiri and Taliban leader Mullah Omar are still kicking around, it's common sense to ask, "How come these guys aren't dead yet?" Silly me, I always thought that if we ever had an actual War on Terror we would begin by killing, oh, I don't know . . . *terrorists*!

When more than 3,000 American service members have given their lives in the War on Terror, it's common sense to wonder how in the world we can still be fighting a lethal insurgency in Iraq, contending with a rejuvenated Taliban in Afghanistan, and watching terrorists launch brutal attacks all over the globe.

When Iran supports the terrorists in Iraq, boasts about its nuclear program, test-fires dozens of long-range missiles, and openly calls for the destruction of Israel, our only true friend in the Middle East, it's common sense to ask how these guys can get away with making the United States look more useless than a eunuch in a whorehouse.

When Hamas, a terrorist group supported by Iran, gets voted into office in the Palestinians' democratic elections, it's common sense to wonder how well we're really doing in the battle for hearts and minds in the Middle East.

When the terrorist group Hezbollah, another Iranian proxy, takes over Lebanon and goes to war against our Israeli allies, it's common sense to start throwing things at the television.

When we're still letting our supposed ally Saudi Arabia fund terrorists, it's common sense to think, "What the hell is this?"

When North Korea gives the world the finger by testing a nuclear bomb and doing whatever else it wants, it's common sense to ask how the bastards can get away with this crap.

When the Russian Mafia is still training and arming anyone who will fork over some cash, including terrorists, it's common sense to think that maybe we're not all that safe yet.

Like I said, recognizing—and speaking honestly about—these lingering problems is just common sense. And so is coming up with solutions.

Let's try some common sense in this book.

TO SERVE AND PROTECT?

The problems we are experiencing—and these problems are legion—have nothing to do with our soldiers, who are doing a great job carrying the load for the rest of us. The problems have everything to do with their leaders, both military and civilian.

If we could find a group of men and women who cared more about getting the job done than how they looked doing their jobs, then the Iraq War would have been over two years ago and the War on Terror would look very different today. Just so we're clear, I'm talking not only about politicians but also about senior officers in the military. Both have forgotten that their job is protecting this nation, not their own asses. If we had the right kind of people in charge—the self*less*, not the selfish—we would have already found and killed bin Laden no matter what country said, "You may not look within our borders."

We'd also be out of Iraq by now because we would have stopped the Syrians, Iranians, and Saudis from interfering. We would have disbanded all the Iraqi militias and killed Muqtada al-Sadr for threatening and killing Americans. We would have fired the top civilian official— the secretary of defense—for his many mistakes much earlier.

If we had accomplished these important strategic imperatives, we would now be in a position to deal much more decisively with Iran, which probably has the real weapon of mass destruction—the bomb— rather than the faux WMDs we insisted were in Iraq. Instead, our great soldiers, sailors, and Marines have been stretched so thin that we can't move them into Iran.

In June 2006, Senator Rick Santorum and Congressman Pete Hoekstra announced that "we have found weapons of mass destruction in Iraq."[3] Oh, really? We found only 500 munitions that contained degrading sarin and mustard gas—and these dated from before 1991. These were not the tons and tons of weapons we were told existed, nor were they *the* WMDs we heard so much about. We didn't go to war and have tens of thousands of soldiers killed and wounded for these leftover, forgotten missiles.

Much of what we do in life is guided by self-interest, and I get that. There are, however, things that should be above all that. There are people out there who do care more about doing things right than about the politics of *looking like* we are doing things right. We stumble across them in every field, including politics and the military. They are the risk takers. They are rare. We need more of them and we need them in positions of authority and power.

Currently, we have a group of leaders in the military, in the bureaucracy, and in elected office who lack the courage to be risk takers. A risk taker is a leader who cares only about the job, getting the mission done, and the men and women he or she leads. Risk takers do not care about how getting the job done affects their careers. They are the outspoken ones. They are the few who will stand up to the boss. They are the ones who will tell the truth no matter who doesn't want to hear it. Without them, we are lost.

Instead of risk takers running this war, we have generals who spend more time planning their next assignment and worrying about their next promotion than figuring out how to fight this war correctly. A true leader cares about only two things: killing bad guys and bringing our boys and girls home in one piece. Fuck the rest!

When the order comes, when the enemy is there, when you know you and your troops are ready—hell, even if you are not ready—you go up the hill, take the town, or attack the beach. It is what you do! You do this knowing that you, or your men, may not make it out in one piece, or back from the fray at all. The willingness to do such things is what makes risk takers and true leaders different.

This goes for leaders in and out of uniform. If you're a leader, you shouldn't worry about your guys getting killed or wounded because it will look bad on your record, hurt your "policy," or, my personal favorite, affect your "legacy." That's playing politics. Unfortunately, that's what we're stuck with way too often. We have these kinds of political players making life-and-death decisions. General Tommy Franks decided not to bring more troops into Afghanistan because he was afraid how it would look if our guys were killed. As a result, bin Laden got away. When we took Baghdad, we needed to shoot looters to establish discipline and control. (Yeah, that's right, I did say shoot looters; we'll get into the reasons why in Chapter 3.) Yet the general and the secretary of defense wouldn't allow it. They wouldn't take the risk. After the successful invasion of Iraq, we needed to get the Iraqis involved in their own security and defense. Instead, we disbanded the entire Iraqi army and police force without training their replacements. This was the premier, numero uno, biggest mistake in a war that has seen us make a boatload of mistakes. This massively, disturbingly stupid decision was the work of the Department of Defense and had to do with political expediency and not angering the Shia.

Our elected officials are, of course, even more concerned with politics. They appear to care more about raising money for their inane political advertising and phony opinion polls than they do about our nation's safety. They care more about which side wins the political battle than they do the real battles. They are definitely not risk takers; they are risk avoiders. When we look at how we are doing in the War on Terror, it appears that we are led by the risk avoiders.

We have an entire government full of self-serving, arrogant, can't-find-their-ass-with-both-hands, unimaginative pretty boys and girls who know only one thing: how to protect their perfumed asses. They are losing this war for us. We can't have our military leaders saying that roadside bombings in Iraq are down when they've actually doubled. We can't have the Pentagon insisting that there's no insurgency in Iraq while our men and women are being killed in one. But oh, that's right; we actually *have* had our leaders feeding us that spin. Sorry, guys; how about the truth for a change?

To borrow the title of one of my favorite books: They Just Don't Get It.

NO POLITICS, NO SPIN

Fighting a war against wild-eyed nut jobs who live in caves and fly planes into buildings is hard enough without the kind of idiocy that we have seen from our elected and appointed leaders. But I guess I shouldn't be surprised. For the past forty years our leaders have been avoiding their responsibilities when it comes to terrorism. Honestly, we would win this war quicker and with less trouble without them.

This really is (or should be) a sergeants' war. Things like house-to-house fighting and driving trucks down dangerous roads are all about sergeants, not generals. The sergeants and their soldiers know what they must do; nor can you question the bravery and excellence of the Special Forces, the Navy SEALs, and the Marines. Their officers only get in their way. That's not to say leaders can't be brave too, but they have agendas, while the soldiers don't.

I don't do politics, agendas, or spin; none of these things interests me. For me, the number one issue is terrorism. None of the other stuff that takes up our time or distracts us from terrorism matters at all. If the bad guys win, the rest of it will be meaningless. We are at war, and while we are at war, we must be focused. Politics is drawing our focus away from where it needs to be. Our focus needs to be on ensuring our survival.

Over the past couple of years we've heard a lot of name-calling from both sides of the political aisle. This isn't helpful either. We need everyone focused on the bad guys. We need everyone to understand that this War on Terror is about survival, not political self-interest. We don't need congressmen like John Murtha using the Marines as whipping posts in order to get on the nightly news, but at the same time, we don't need former Marines like Murtha, who fought in two wars, being called cowards and traitors. We don't need senators with foot-in-mouth disease saying that Guantanamo is like a Russian gulag. The prisoners in Gitmo live better than most prisoners in jails within the United States. Hell, they live better than the guards!

We also don't need disgruntled government employees sharing our secrets with the press. There are at least three covert or secret programs that ain't secret no more because they have been spread all over the front page of the *New York Times.* Now, my first instinct is to blame the press, but the truth is that without the traitors who give up these secrets, there would be nothing to publish. As for the media, the reality is this: every once in a while, it really is okay to be an American first. It's okay to think of others and not to do something just because you *can* do it. Every once in a while, when the government calls and asks you not to publish something because it will damage a secret program and endanger national security, it's okay not to do it. Our government, for as many mistakes as it makes and will continue to make, sometimes gets it right. Every once in a while we can stop being self-promoting assholes and take one for the damn team. In case you need to be reminded, that team is the United States of America.

All of these things hurt the war effort, but not in the way you might think. It isn't giving aid and comfort to the enemy to express ideas different from those held by the people in charge. In this, the best damn country in the world, dissent is one way we maintain our edge. Dissent doesn't embolden terrorists; the only thing that does is not killing the bastards. Dissenters don't contribute to the death and maiming of American soldiers—not even the biggest loudmouths, like the fat and over-the-top Michael Moore, the very loud and very wrong Howard Dean, and Ted "I-can't-believe-I-ate-the-whole-thing" Kennedy. But this kind of bickering *does* hurt the war effort, because it requires us to stop what we're doing to deal with politics. We are spending way too much time and energy fighting each other instead of fighting al-Qaeda.

STOPPING AT NOTHING

What *really* hurts our war effort are leaders who won't deal with reality. We need to unify the government into an iron fist of will that will stop at nothing to defeat this enemy.

I figured that after 9/11, which was the predictable result of ignoring terrorism for forty years, we would have hunted down and killed the bastards responsible for the horrific attacks. After 9/11, I *knew* that we wouldn't allow politics to dictate how we fought these guys, and that we'd bring to bear the full force and power of the United States— diplomatic, economic, and, when necessary, military power—on those countries that directly sponsored terrorism. I was also sure that we would finally get serious about stopping the sponsors of terrorism. I knew we'd publicly denounce Wahhabism, the most militant strain of Islam and the state-sponsored religion of Saudi Arabia. Then, I was certain, we'd stop buying oil from the Saudis until they denounced it as well. We might even take an oil farm from them by force as payment for all of the help we've given them in the past. I knew we wouldn't deal with them as friends until they got serious about stopping terrorism in their own country.

I was wrong on all counts. We've done none of that. Terrorists from bin Laden down to Iraqi militia leader Muqtada al-Sadr haven't been killed. Politics and butt covering have kept us from fighting this war right. Saudi Arabia gets away with its policies because we allow it. It's time to stop this nonsense.

In this book I'm going to show you how we can fix our mistakes and put this war on the right track. The key thing will be to change our mind-set almost completely. Forget risk avoidance and covering our butts. We need to focus on survival. The suggestions may not always sound pretty, but that doesn't mean we should run away from them. We can't, because we need to do what *works,* not what sounds good or wins us kudos from the politically correct crowd.

Take the state sponsors of terrorism, countries like Iran, Lebanon, Syria, Pakistan, and all the rest. How do we deal with them? Well, I'll tell you one thing for damn sure: whatever we've been doing hasn't been working. We should have tried to get countries that support terrorism to start working with us before 9/11, but we didn't. We should have started right after 9/11, but we didn't do it then either. We had best do it now. And there are ways we can get results, fast. How about we park a carrier task force in the Mediterranean and bomb the piss out of Syria's intelligence and military headquarters, and then every time we catch another Syrian operation hurting us, we drop another bomb? That might make the Syrians think twice, don't you think?

And while we are doing that, we should also get the attention of those who indirectly support terrorism, countries like Canada, with its domestic-terrorist-friendly policies, and France and Germany, which do business with terrorist-friendly nations. Every week, we are treated to yet another revelation that our neighbors and "friends" are not acting like our allies. When this happens, we should tell them: no imports, no jobs, no technology, at least not until you start acting like our friends. We have this massive economic engine; how about we use it?

And what about dealing with the terrorists themselves? For starters, how about having an *honest* conversation about the threats we're facing? Sounds pretty basic, right? Then why can't our government frankly acknowledge the cultural and religious realities of this war and this enemy? We can't even admit that this is a religious war because of all of the political correctness championed by the talking heads.

If this isn't a religious war, then what the hell is it? We are being attacked by terrorists trained in religious schools called madrassas. We are being attacked by Wahhabists, followers of the most violent form of Islam. Bin Laden has declared a jihad, or holy war, against us. What part of "religious war" don't we understand? We can talk about the complexities of the issues all we want, and get into a serious theological conversation about the true nature of Islam. But that's kind of beside the point. The very real truth, the unavoidable truth, is that at least half of the Muslim world hates us.

Hey, so they hate us—fine with me. But it's essential that we know it and *deal with it*. It's important to our very existence that we know and understand the hatred and the reasons behind it so that we can combat it, defeat it, and, if possible, change it.

If we had done things right from the beginning, we would have bases up and running in Iraq and an economy that was putting Iraqis to work doing something besides building roadside bombs. We would have an Army and Marine Corps that were rested and ready to take on Iran if necessary. We would have had time to go into Pakistan to find and kill bin Laden. We would have put in the time, money, weaponry, and men and women to finish the Taliban the first time and dealt with Afghanistan correctly from the outset.

Somehow it seems we have forgotten what happened to us just a few short years ago when on a beautiful fall morning more Americans were killed than died at Pearl Harbor; when men and women chose to throw themselves out of the Twin Towers rather than burn to death; when every airport in the country was shut down; when we learned to our horror that we were no longer safe, that the ocean and our arrogance would no longer protect us. This is the big mistake we've made— not just our leaders, but all of us.

We have for sure forgotten that this war is all over the world, not just in Iraq. We have accepted the next attack, and that means we have already lost. Not the way to win a war, methinks.

CHAPTER 2

GETTING THE WAR ON TERROR RIGHT

The face of the War on Terror, for most U.S. citizens, is Iraq. The president has said that Iraq is where the terrorists have chosen to make their stand, and this, to some extent, is true. The whole truth, however, is that the terrorists have chosen to make their stand in Iraq because *we* are there.

The War on Terror was never supposed to be a guerilla war. After the initial assault on Afghanistan, the War on Terror was supposed to be a war fought mostly in the shadows. It was supposed to be a war fought with spies, intelligence, and Special Forces that operated behind the scenes, in mountains and in caves. It was supposed to be fought in boardrooms against corrupt banks and in the government buildings of corrupt regimes. It was supposed to be fought in back alleys and dank, mildew-smelling hotel rooms where terrorists dwell. It was also supposed to be fought in your hometown where the terrorists hide.

Instead of fighting the War on Terror that way, which is the right way, we went to Iraq in search of weapons of mass destruction that weren't there. As a result, we are now fighting against an insurgency in a country where we are viewed as occupiers. This is the war we see and hear about on the evening news, but the war we were supposed to fight still awaits us. This face we have painted on the War on Terror, Iraq, will be discussed in a later chapter. But if you really want to know where we stand in the War on Terror, you can't begin by looking only at Iraq; you have to start with the broader picture, the global picture— the *actual* War on Terror.

FINISHING THE JOB IN AFGHANISTAN

The offensive in the War on Terror began in Afghanistan. Why? Osama bin Laden, the architect of 9/11, was there. Ayman al-Zawahiri, al-Qaeda's number two man, was there. Mullah Omar and the Taliban were there. Al-Qaeda training camps were there and 9/11 was planned, rehearsed, and coordinated from there. It was the right, proper, and po- etically just place to drop CIA and Special Forces, which, with some help from the Air Force, initiated the War on Terror.

Man, we at least started that one right! We sent 350 Special Forces soldiers and 110 CIA officers armed with satellite radios and bags of money to buy up our momentary friends, the Northern Alliance, to help us take back Afghanistan for the good guys. In a matter of weeks the place was ours. According to both me and the head CIA guy on the ground in Afghanistan, we had bin Laden and al-Zawahiri cornered in Tora Bora. All we had to do was go and get them. We also had Mullah Omar in our sights. We were righteous; we were beautiful.[1]

But before we could get it done, the colonels and paper pushers ar- rived with their PowerPoint briefings and conference calls and, true to form, hedged at taking risks. Up until that point, the United States had been successful in fighting the Taliban because Gary Berntsen, the CIA head of operations who led the invasion of Afghanistan with the Spe- cial Forces guys, was willing to take calculated risks. The colonels, of course, were not.

To make matters worse, the generals and CENTCOM (Central Command) also got involved. We had bin Laden and al-Zawahiri cor- nered in a cave in Tora Bora and we let them go! Berntsen repeatedly requested 900 Rangers to block the escape routes bin Laden used, but he was turned down and then transferred out of Afghanistan. General Tommy Franks was the CENTCOM commander and he was, for sure, the guy in charge. He was the one who made the decision not to send in the additional soldiers being requested. Jesus, General, what do you do for a living? Your job was so simple—support the guys on the ground—and you blew it. Dammit, this is just plain bullshit. You should be ashamed of yourself.

When asked why he refused to send in the 900 Rangers that had been requested, Franks said, "I was very mindful of the Soviet experience of more than ten years, having introduced 620,000 troops into Afghanistan, more than 15,000 of them being killed, more than 55,000 of them being wounded."[2] Hey, General, we are at war and we are not the Soviets! This was your chance to take a risk and you blew it, and because you blew it, the head of al-Qaeda got away. Nice going; hope you are enjoying your book and lecture tour.

Read Gary Berntsen's book, *Jawbreaker,* to see just how much can be accomplished by real leaders and risk takers, as well as what can be lost by politicians and military leaders who are only concerned with covering their asses.

What was lost? Well, bin Laden, of course, to name a big one. In January 2005 he released one of his famous tapes, this one taunting us by saying that we wouldn't take him alive. Fine with me; I'd rather kill him! Problem is, we still can't find him. It's bad enough that we let this terrorist master go, but it's even worse when he calls on the Shia in Iraq to kill the Sunnis, as he did in a June 2006 tape. We don't need any help creating bedlam in Iraq. It is long past time we silence this guy.

In September 2006 bin Laden was being touted as dead—again. This time he supposedly succumbed to typhus. Five years after 9/11, we don't know if the man ultimately responsible is dead or alive. Bin Laden is still a symbol of power to terrorists. The only way to diminish him is to kill him. Instead, we keep making things up about this murderer: he is on dialysis, he is dying, he is dead, he is not in power, he is not the leader of al-Qaeda. All of this is crap. Truth is, we have no earthly idea where he is, what he is doing, whether he is sleeping, awake, taking a dump, whatever. As my sainted father would say, "We know *bupkis*."

We also lost Zawahiri at Tora Bora. In January 2006, we lost him again and instead killed eighteen people and some cows in Pakistan but missed the real target. That led to two taunting tapes from Zawahiri saying, "You missed me. You missed me." How is it that we can cure pimples, invent the iPod, and still not be able to find one fifty-four-year-old Egyptian doctor who every few weeks comes on world television and says, "Fuck You"?

The bottom line is that we didn't finish the job in Afghanistan. If we had wanted to do Afghanistan right, as soon as the Taliban fell we would have pushed on wherever the trail led us and captured bin Laden. But that would have been just the beginning. The truth is that in Afghanistan we were pitifully underprepared for our predictable victory, just as we'd later be unprepared in Iraq. It has always been the case that keeping a peace is harder than winning a war, and we should have known that and prepared for it. We did not. The United States has not had a coordinated government effort on this war for one single day.

Right behind the Special Forces and CIA guys we should have had a full deployment of people from the Department of State and every other government agency, working almost shoulder to shoulder with the military to rebuild the country and win the hearts and minds of the Afghan people. We needed trucks full of money, trainers, builders, security troops, teachers, clerics, nurses, doctors, and bureaucrats to immediately start helping the people of Afghanistan so that they might take advantage of the country we had given back to them.

Some people believe that U.S. military troops shouldn't be responsible for rebuilding Afghanistan. In fact, from the time he took charge Secretary of Defense Donald Rumsfeld pointedly said that "nation building" would not be part of the mandate of what he viewed as the "new" military. This sounds nice—sure, we don't want to have our fighting forces stuck endlessly somewhere overseas doing jobs that are unnecessary. But this knee-jerk aversion to so-called nation building has gotten us in a huge amount of trouble. Think about it: what happens if we *don't* rebuild Afghanistan? I'll tell you what: the Taliban will come back.

Oh, wait, I'm sorry, the Taliban already *have* come back. That's right—because we did not allow our soldiers to do the job right the first time, the Taliban came back with a vengeance. One of the reasons for their return is that we did not kill Taliban leader Mullah Omar. According to my CIA, FBI, Special Forces, and SEAL contacts, he is believed to be on the Afghan side of the border between Pakistan and Afghanistan, opposite Waziristan. He is thought to be very active, especially in directing the Taliban's resurgence in southern Afghanistan. He has not only gathered remnants of the former Taliban under his leadership but he also recruited new members from the madrassas in Pakistan. He has started poisoning and corrupting a whole new generation who plan to outlast us, and then take over the government once again.[3]

What happened when the Taliban gathered strength? Teachers, schoolkids, doctors, and nurses were beaten and beheaded, schools were blown apart, and all the while the good guys did little to stop the violence. With the Taliban resurgent, we were finally forced, in mid-2006, to launch another major military offensive in southern Afghanistan: Operation Mountain Thrust (and no, I don't know why many military campaigns have sexual innuendo all over their titles). This was, in fact, the largest military offensive in Afghanistan yet, featuring more than 10,000 troops, most of them American.

The campaign was two years late in coming, but at least it finally happened. Now the job needs to be completed. Most NATO countries have failed to fulfill their troop commitments, the guy in charge over there has said we need 30,000 more troops to complete the mission, and most of the soldiers already there have been restricted from going into "danger zones." Then, in late November 2006, the military decided to allow these forces to move into southern Afghanistan to fight the Taliban when there are emergencies. Let me tell you this; anytime the Taliban is controlling any part of a country, we are experiencing an emergency. Hopefully, this revised tactical decision will correct the past wrongs of the operation. Because if we don't finish the job in

Afghanistan, the Afghan people will say that the United States cannot be trusted. Whatever hope and belief in democracy they may have had will be shattered and they will join the Taliban and al-Qaeda in even greater numbers. Then, when and if we have to go back to get bin Laden or the next powerful terrorist leader hiding there, we cannot expect any help from the Afghan people.

When we joined this War on Terror and invaded countries like Afghanistan and Iraq, we were obligated to fix them, not only morally but from a practical standpoint as well. If we do otherwise, we cannot possibly hope to win this war. So we soldier on and do "nation building." It sucks. It costs lives and boatloads of money, but there is no other way. If you take a country, you must fix a country.

So why aren't we fixing it yet? Why are we fighting against ourselves? Fighting against yourself is a good idea only when you are in a gym, doing resistance training trying to build big muscles. It is never a good idea in a war. Yet here we are, still working against ourselves by rotating our on-the-ground guys in and out of Afghanistan every second. Even though we need right-now-on-the-ground-happening intelligence, we're sending in CIA personnel on ninety-day tours, and our State Department guys are assigned there for no more than six months. In ninety days, some people in the CIA can't even locate their position on a map, never mind build relationships with the people in that country. In six months, State Department employees barely have time to unpack their paper clips before it is time to come home.

We need a change in assignment policy. CIA and State Department personnel should be assigned to these places for a minimum of one year—just like in the military. When all the government agencies that are designed to fight this war are not on the same page, or not even in the same damn book, then we are fighting this war with both hands tied behind our back. The result will be failure.

We also have not finished the training of the Afghan army and police forces. This is difficult and dangerous work, mostly being done by American private contractors. As of July 2006 we had trained 30,000 troops, but that's not enough—not enough by a factor of ten.[4]

One of my great friends, a former college buddy who is retired Army Special Forces, is in Afghanistan helping to train the new Afghan army. He is struggling to convey the nature of leadership and ethics to uneducated tribesmen who think not only that it's okay to kill their wife or daughter if she is adulterous but that it's *required*. This is a challenge, to say the least. The Afghan people are tough, but they are massively independent, which is not a great trait for an army. They are also dirt poor and easily bought, and they have a tendency to stop fighting and go home.

On top of those kinds of obstacles, the new Afghan military faces a severe lack of competence on the part of their government. The government can't equip, house, or pay the trained troops it has. We trained 35,000 policemen, but we can't equip them with guns either. These are essential ingredients in the "nation building" within Afghanistan. To say our efforts have been ineffective is a huge understatement.

The truth is that the Afghan military is not something we can fix in this lifetime. Without the Americans there, the army doesn't exist; it is just a bunch of guys we trained who will go home. We knew this—or should have known this. You can't take a group of people with a stone-age mentality and turn them into a military force in a short period of time. We have learned this from experience. For example, we have been in South Korea, training its armed forces, for more than fifty years and they are still not even close to our standards of fighting. We knew this but weren't honest about it, and now everyone is paying for it.

Given all this, it's no surprise that we've failed miserably when it comes to disbanding and gaining control of the militias. Afghanistan has 65,000 to 80,000 militia members roaming around. This makes any of our efforts to venture into more and more of the country too dangerous. The reality is that the country is slipping out of our control. (Want to see how bad things have gotten? Take a look at the map of Afghanistan in the Appendix, on page 180.)

Another clear demonstration of our failure at "nation building" in Afghanistan is the fact that we didn't even come close to shutting down the country's drug trade. In fact, opium production has *grown* since we launched military operations in 2001. In 2000, Afghanistan cultivated 82,000 hectares of poppy, which yields opium; in 2001 that number dropped to just 8,000 hectares, but by 2006 it had climbed to 165,000 hectares, a record high.[5] Afghanistan now supplies more than 90 *percent* of the world's opium.[6] Care to guess who its biggest importer is? Yup, that would be the United States.

This is truly unbelievable. The NATO commander, a damn good man, is saying we've got trouble, big trouble, in Afghanistan; the drug czar is saying it; the director of the CIA is saying it. It's a sad day when we're hearing these things from our leaders, five years after we supposedly took control of Afghanistan.

We are fighting the War on Terror the same way we fight the war on drugs—which is to say, really badly. Afghanistan has become a narcotics state with lots of corruption and tons of money floating around. Hell, the brother of Afghanistan's president is a known drug kingpin. The real problem with all of this is that the money from drug trafficking is being funneled to terrorists right under our noses, and we either can't or won't stop it. If this is the best we can do, then we should leave.

Afghanistan did not focus. We diffused. We splintered. We screwed up in a huge way. At a time when our focus needed to be X-ray-vision clear, we were distracted by bad intelligence that had been gathered by incompetent people who were more concerned with politics than with our safety. Instead of finishing the job in Afghanistan, we turned our sights on Iraq.

THE NORTH KOREAN DANGER

It might be possible, although I doubt it, to excuse our ineffective efforts when dealing with Afghanistan if we had solved a whole range of other problems we have recently faced around the globe. But that is not the case. Witness the biggest threat we face, North Korea. It is a country run by a nut job who has nuclear bombs and other deadly weapons. The Pentagon says that North Korea has "stockpiles of chemical weapons and can produce nerve and asphyxiation gases in bulk. North Korea is also thought to have an active but primitive biological weapons program, which violates international treaties and might be able to produce anthrax, cholera, and plague."[7] If that doesn't freak you out just a little, it should! North Korea also has missiles that could reach the western United States.

In October 2006 the North Koreans gave us a good sense of why we should be freaked out. Once again they gave the entire world the finger, this time by conducting an underground nuclear explosive test. This came just a few months after they test-fired seven missiles, defying strong warnings from the United States and other countries not to do so. Strong warnings? We yelled at them and made speeches and then did nothing. In the end, they called our bluff and fired the missiles. We did nothing again, thus displaying the awesome power and influence of the United States of America.

If you aren't sick yet, you should be. The CIA's best guess as to whether North Korea has the technology to arm those missiles with WMDs is . . . they don't know. Isn't that comforting?

In case you aren't disgusted yet, try this. When North Korea was shooting missiles into the Sea of Japan in the summer of 2006, guess who was invited to watch? Iran. And the Iranians showed up too.

The North Koreans sell all manner of bad things to any nation on the face of the planet with the money to buy them. They sell missiles, guns, technology, and enriched uranium to any and all that wish to buy them. They have sold ballistic missile technology to countries that the State Department lists as sponsors of terrorism—Iran, Syria, Pakistan, and Yemen. Such technology could be used to deliver chemical, biological, and nuclear weapons. Such sales are the primary source of hard currency for this isolated country, and the proceeds allow North Korea to fund its own missile programs.

A few years ago the North Koreans perfected the counterfeiting of U.S. currency to the point that the U.S. Treasury Department could not discern the forgeries. North Korea uses this phony-money capability to buy things and undermine governments. They teamed up with Iran to make the forgery, using German technology—ultrasensitive, powerful reproduction machines, high-quality printers, very expensive paper, and enough computers to fill a ten-story building. The forgery was so perfect that our government had to make another series of $50 and $100 bills with holographic images on them. Anyone care to guess how much money this cost our government? The answer is no one knows.

The North Koreans have been out of control for decades. They have been destroyers of their own people, they are exporters of terror, and they have been on the ass end of badness. They are evil personified. They have to be dealt with sooner rather than later.[8]

We have four possibilities when it comes to dealing with North Korea. One, we can do what we are doing now, which is little or nothing. Two, we can go to war with North Korea, but only with our Air Force, Navy aviators, and cruise missiles; if we do this, however, South Korea will be toast. Three, we can keep threatening them and not follow through, thus showing the world over and over that we don't mean what we say. Or four, we can talk to them. We can get China and Russia involved and make a deal—a business deal. North Korea has been on the verge of collapse for decades. There are no dogs or cats alive there 'cause they've all been eaten; that's how bad things are. It is time to play Let's Make a Deal.

If our government were working right, North Korea wouldn't have the bomb or be selling weapons to terrorist groups and threatening annihilation of their neighbor to the south. We'd see a treaty-signing ceremony, pictures of Americans feeding starving Koreans, and demonstrable evidence that North Korea has taken our advice and knocked off the crap about building nukes and helping terrorists. What we wouldn't see, and wouldn't need to see, is what happened behind closed doors to make those achievements happen.

How do you do a backroom deal with another country? Just ask the Mafia; they've been making these kinds of deals with Italian and American politicians for decades. Or we could ask al-Qaeda; they are still making backroom deals with Saudi Arabia and Pakistan. It's really not that difficult, and it's how bad guys are used to doing business.

Sure, we aren't the bad guys, but when you're fighting for your very survival, sometimes you need to do what works—especially when everything you've tried has been proven to be worth less than a bucket of warm piss.

When it comes to North Korea, the deal gets made by the Chinese or Russians, both massively corrupt societies and governments. At least sometimes, we can make that corruption work in our favor. We could bribe a Belgian arms dealer to make an offer to a senior Chinese government official to meet with the North Koreans and get them to meet with U.S. representatives or private industry types—big names that everyone would recognize, the kind of former top U.S. officials who are used to high-level negotiations. We let the North Koreans pick the country. We meet without an agenda, without entourages and staffs—two from each side plus one interpreter—and we talk. We find out what it will take to make the North Koreans do the things we want, like stop developing nuclear weapons and giving aid to terrorists. In return, we will guarantee loans, give boatloads of humanitarian aid, and help develop industry to help begin to make North Korea solvent.

This hasn't happened because we aren't fighting it right. How do we know that? Because in September 2005, the North Koreans agreed to give up all nuclear activities and rejoin the Nuclear Non-proliferation Treaty. Twelve hours later, they changed their minds. What a surprise! How shocked are we all? Oh, and not only did they change their minds, they also demanded we give them a light-water nuclear reactor.[9]

Then, in late 2005, North Korea sold eighteen BM-25 missiles to the Islamic Republic of Iran, another deadly threat to the United States and our allies that we're not properly dealing with. According to the German intelligence services, Iranian experts are already working on fitting the North Korean missiles with nuclear warheads.[10]

Oh, don't forget that Iranian president Mahmoud Ahmadinejad has declared that "Israel must be wiped off the map."[11] The range of the missiles Iran bought from North Korea is 3,500 kilometers—that gets them to Israel, and parts of Western Europe too.[12]

THE IRANIAN FANATICS

Remember the "Axis of Evil"? The president used that phrase in his 2002 State of the Union address to describe North Korea, Iran, and Iraq. The North Korean missile deal demonstrates how these rogue states do sometimes cooperate. But even working on its own, Iran represents a major danger. The War on Terror—a *real* War on Terror— can't ignore Iran because since the Islamic Revolution of 1979, Iran has been one of the top three state sponsors of terrorism.

Iran is a country run by religious fanatics who preach hatred toward Westerners and openly call for the destruction of Israel. Iran has given money, training, equipment, national intelligence support, and, of course, safe haven to a variety of terrorist organizations—Hamas, the majority Palestinian political party and freely elected representatives of the Palestinian people; Hezbollah, an organization of radical Shia Muslims that controls more than thirty seats in the Lebanese parliament and in 2006 spent thirty-four days at war with Israel; and the Islamic Brotherhood, a worldwide Islamist conservative movement.

In 1979, Iranian radicals captured fifty-two Americans and held them hostage for 444 days in Iran. Among the leaders of the student organization that planned the Tehran embassy takeover, the Office of Strengthening Unity, was the current president of Iran, Ahmadinejad.[13] In 1983, Hezbollah—with funding and approval from Iran—killed 241 U.S. Marines in a suicide bombing in Beirut.[14] More recently, the Iranians have provided safe haven to members of al-Qaeda, funneled money, arms, and other support to the militias in Iraq, and announced that they will not allow us to monitor their nuclear activities.[15]

We believe Iran has more than thirty-five sites devoted to building a nuclear capability. The truth is that Iran probably already has the bomb but not the capability for delivering it on a missile or the device to trigger the bomb.[16] But it is trying to get those capabilities, and we know it. We also know that A. Q. Khan (the former head of the Pakistan nuclear program), the Russians, the Chinese, and the North Koreans—not a nice group—are helping them.

In July 2002, representatives of the world's top terrorist organizations met in Tehran. More than a hundred of the world's most wanted men or their proxies were in attendance. Iranian officials described the conference, called Ten Days of Dawn, as a leadership summit focused on "cultural and informational activities." But in fact, the purpose of the conference was to plot out how to kill us. One of the planned "informational activities" was training offered by the Islamic Revolutionary Guards. The brochure presented this training as "courses in self-defense."[17]

The trend in the Middle East since 2003 has been cooperation among terrorist organizations, which means that in many cases the bad guys have put aside their differences to wage a jihad against Israel and the "Western infidels." That means that Hezbollah, Hamas, Fatah-Tanzim (the armed wing of Al'Fatah), and the Popular Front (national Palestinian political military organization) are now at war against Israel and her perceived or real allies to further the Islamo-fascist cause. Although United Nations Resolution 1559 called for disarmament of all Lebanese and non-Lebanese militias, the government is unable to control the Syrian- and Iranian-sponsored Hezbollah. Even the secretary-general of the United Nations in a report to the Security Council called for the end of interference from Syria and Iran.[18]

Now we are really getting our face rubbed in it. Iran's surrogate in the terrorism business, Hamas, has taken control of the Palestinian territories. The Iranians have been all over the world on TV, at conferences, and on the radio yelling that Israel should not exist, the Holocaust never happened, and oh, by the way, they have the bomb and they aren't going to stop making it.

The United States is trying diplomacy and we'd better hope it works because right now, given our focus on Afghanistan and Iraq, there is little we can do about this situation militarily. Unfortunately, everyone, including the Iranians, knows this.

So how should we deal with Iran? We've already decided that military action is not possible at this time. We can call Ahmadinejad a terrorist—oops, we already did that, and it didn't help. We are doing some things right, mainly by continuing to support Israel in its fight against Hezbollah, which gets most of its weapons and money from Iran's Revolutionary Guards, and which one high-level Iranian official called "one of the pillars of our security strategy."[19] So our major line of defense against the Iranian terrorist state must be aiding Israel's efforts to cut off Hezbollah from Syrian and Iranian resupply and reinforcement, and continuing our diplomatic efforts to ensure an independent Lebanon that is no longer at the mercy of its neighbors.

SYRIA'S TERRORIST CONNECTION

Another of the problem spots around the globe is Syria, which neighbors the nation where we have been fighting a ground war since 2003. If our government worked right, Vice President Cheney would go behind closed doors, stick his finger in the chest of President Assad, and tell him that the next time a Syrian terrorist son of a bitch crosses the border and kills one of our guys in Iraq, Syria's National Intelligence Board—its CIA equivalent, which is propping up terrorists—will be leveled by the U.S. Air Force. All we'd see on the news was the rubble that used to be the National Intelligence Board. And all we'd read in the *New York Times* was how Syria is demonstrating new commitment to helping us stabilize Iraq "in the interest of peace."

But our government's strategy is not working because terrorists are crossing the Syrian border and blowing up our guys in Iraq at an alarming rate. It is time to try it my way.

When I talk about "my way," I'm not talking about buying the support of a whole country; these backroom deals are made directly with the leadership of countries, or at least a few people high up in the government. The self-interest of these leaders will be to our advantage. We can make deals with Syria, but no one is going to go out and announce that Syria and the United States are now the best of friends and will support each other in all they do. In exchange for buying these people we get subtle things. The result of the deals I am talking about are small. For example, arms and bad guys stop going over the border into Iraq, or a more pro-U.S. guy gets appointed to the top military or intelligence position. It is not as flashy as announcing that Syria is going to install a Western-style democracy, but it is way more effective. It's time to talk to someone in Syria and appeal to his self-interest, because I will tell you this: if we can't figure out how to deal with Syria, then the North Koreas and Irans of this world will always be a bridge too far.

Sometimes we pay people or give them what they want and then just wait until another opportunity comes along to get what we want. We make deals and do things that will not be well received by other countries or the American people. We get our hands dirty because that is what it takes to win this kind of war.

WITH FRIENDS LIKE THESE . . .

You might think it is just badass countries in the Middle East and Asia we can't or won't deal with, but this isn't the case. In reality, most of the time we don't even know what to do with our friends.

Few countries can rival pompous France for pure unadulterated arrogance and hatred of anything and everything American. The French worked against us in the Balkans by helping both sides and interfering with our efforts. They have consistently worked against us in Africa by voting in the United Nations against every single effort to help stop the slaughter in Sudan. They sold anti-tank missiles to Iraq, missiles that actually killed Americans. They helped Saddam build bombproof bunkers even we could not penetrate. They are corrupt to the core. They have great spies, great soldiers, big doors, lousy cheese, and a hatred for us that clouds their judgment.

What kind of penalty have we levied on the French for their treacherous behavior? *Nothing!* How about instead of doing nothing, we nail their prissy asses to the public awareness wall? One word from the president, one phrase like "The French suck" or something similar, will get the world's attention. We could then begin the process of another war, this time one of words. Truth be told, the French need us.

They need us to hate and blame, for sure, but they need our protection the same way the rest of the world does, and they need our money, goods, and services.

France is not our only supposed friend that hurts our efforts in the War on Terror. There is no country that more fits the phrase "With friends like these, who needs enemies?" than Canada. In October 2003 the Security Intelligence Agency, Canada's version of the CIA, issued a report, without blushing, that says Canada's asylum policies and immigration policies make Canada a state very friendly to terrorists. "Canada is viewed by some terrorist groups as a place to try to seek refuge, raise funds, procure materials and/or conduct other support activities," the report notes. "Virtually all of the most notorious international terrorist organizations are known to maintain a network presence in Canada."[20] The intelligence agency identifies some fifty known terrorist groups, including al-Qaeda, that have a presence inside Canada's borders.[21] After 9/11, we know how dangerous this can be.

If we can't figure out how to get Canada to really cooperate with us, how in the heat of desert hell are we going to handle Iran or North Korea?

We must engage the Canadians and convince them to become a more involved ally in this War on Terror. We must get Canada to increase its defense and intelligence forces and become more aggressive. When the Canadians decide to fight, they are awesome. Their snipers saved many American lives in Tora Bora, but our countries are so mad at each other that the Canadian government actually refused medals from us for their soldiers.

Canada in 2006 had a terrorist scare that should have shaken up its government and its citizens enough to make them realize that it's not just their neighbor to the south who is in this fight against the bad guys. Twenty-plus Canadian citizens were arrested before they killed anyone, but they were found to have all manner of killing devices. So now is a good time to offer the Canadians a deal: we will buy more of their stuff—import snow or something—and in return they will act like a real allied nation and help out the rest of the world. Given the recent scare, the Canadians might be more open to the idea of coming on board in this fight.

Time to have a heart-to-heart with Canada.

WINNING HEARTS AND MINDS

There are other countries and regions where extremism and terrorism are just starting to take hold. We have a chance to win the hearts and minds of these people before they join the ranks of those who seek to kill us, but we aren't doing nearly enough.

Indonesia is a chain of more than 17,000 islands off the southeastern coast of Asia that has a population that is 85 percent Muslim. Like many other poor countries, Indonesia has a weak and corrupt government and a loosely regulated financial system. All these things make it a perfect haven for terrorists. In the past, Indonesia was largely a secular society whose citizens practiced a moderate form of Islam, but radical Islamists have been gaining momentum there. Right now we need to be knee-deep in the building of schools and hospitals within Indonesia. By doing so, we would be showing them that we are the good guys. We need to be doing anything and everything to help our image in every way possible.

If you don't think this kind of stuff makes a difference, if you don't think it is a good way to be spending our money, you are wrong. After a tsunami wreaked havoc in Indonesia in late 2004, the White House pledged nearly $1 billion in aid, and American citizens donated another $800 million.[22] Through the United States Agency for International Development (USAID), we helped provide food and water in the days immediately after the disaster. We are now bringing them loans and expertise to help rebuild the country. It has made a difference in the way Indonesians think about the United States and our citizens.

A poll conducted by Terror Free Tomorrow a year after the tsunami shows how we are winning hearts and minds:

- More Indonesians were favorable to the United States than were unfavorable—a huge change from a few years earlier, when only 15 percent of Indonesians held a favorable view.
- Sixty-three percent specifically cited the American response to the tsunami as fostering a more favorable opinion of the United States.
- Support for bin Laden plummeted from 58 percent in 2003 to only 12 percent.
- Sympathy for terrorism in general virtually disappeared, as just 2 percent of Indonesians said they felt suicide terrorist attacks are ever justified—this down from 27 percent after September 11.[23]

There is a lesson to be learned from this experience. We could apply the techniques we used in disaster relief within the Middle Eastern countries where we face grave opposition. It would certainly relieve the occupation image that the Iraq war has fostered.

THE AFRICAN CHALLENGE

We need to focus on Africa as well, and in the good-news category, we are beginning to do just that. We are finally beginning to understand that in these impoverished, HIV-ridden, and just plain hideous conditions, extremist ideology can easily take hold. Life is so bad in much of Africa that anyone who brings money and the promise of something better will receive cooperation from these people. The extremists are buying safe haven and recruits with money and perverted hope.

There are a few U.S. Army Special Forces and some U.S. Marines training troops in Africa (Mali, Ethiopia, Djibouti, and others). The purpose of this training is twofold—help the Africans get better and allow us to spy on the bad guys. We have also made some strategic fixes. It used to be that the State Department had the final say in whether or not U.S. Army Green Berets could be deployed in embassies to help fight the War on Terror. That is no longer the case. Now, Special Forces can be deployed and all they have to do is inform, not ask permission from, the State Department. It is a huge deal and about damn time. So Africa is a work in progress, but at least we are getting started there. We recently went back into Somalia to hunt down those responsible for the two embassy bombings in 1998—finally some aggressive action.

LET'S FIGURE THIS OUT

The task before us is daunting, but there's no way around it; we're in a global war, after all. Notice I said "global war," not "global struggle against violent extremism." That was the ridiculous phrase our government trotted out back in July 2005. "Global struggle against violent extremism"? What the hell is that? Fortunately, we didn't hear too much about this one after Defense Secretary Donald Rumsfeld used the phrase and was almost laughed out of the room.

But the government's aborted PR effort underscores a disturbing point: this terrorism thing is serious stuff and we are not treating it that way. Hell, for that moment in 2005 it seemed pretty clear that our government didn't even want to be in a war anymore. Well, too bad— these threats are real, and deadly. And yet the truth is we haven't demonstrated the political will necessary to deal with the threats. We are good at the small stuff—the getting-distracted stuff, the let's-hold-a-press-conference-and-look-like-we're-being-effective stuff—but we aren't good at the *real* stuff.

As an example of getting distracted and not focusing on the real stuff, consider the press conference the attorney general and the director of the FBI held in June 2006 hailing the capture of an al-Qaeda terrorist cell. Great—except that the ones captured weren't al-Qaeda. The seven young men were more like a Boy Scout troop gone bad or a hip-hop band in fatigues. These misguided, out-of-work, poor black guys were out at midnight in a neighborhood, marching. They were hubcap stealers, maybe gangbangers, but al-Qaeda they were not. I'm glad they're off the street, but come on, there are real terrorists out there. We need to find the real ones, not the ones marching around in fatigues and holding secret meetings in a shed.

We aren't good at direct dialogue with countries that support terrorism because we are afraid of how it will look and what others will think. We aren't good at the necessary killing part of this war because we are afraid of repercussions; we are afraid the rest of the world will think we're too aggressive. But the truth is, we have to be unapologetically aggressive and we have to say it out loud. It's time to admit that we can't have it both ways—win the war *and* look like nice guys doing it.

This if-we-kill-too-many-people-of-one-group-it-will-look-bad or if-we-kill-their-leaders-they'll-kill-ours mentality ties our hands and is bullshit. Killing is part of war. We have to say it, we have to mean it, and we have to do it—without restraint.

We also need more military. Our current forces are exhausted. Additional forces will be costly. In fact, it will cost $15 billion per new division and probably require at least a conversation about the draft. In case we still want to blame someone else—like Clinton—for this one, keep in mind that in the five years since the current administration took charge, the size of the military has increased by only 10,000 members. That is not nearly enough, particularly since some 25,000 have been killed and wounded. Sounds like a minus to me.[24] In 2006, Congress authorized 30,000 more troops, but when the Defense Department's budget came out in 2007 there was no money for them. The budget also cut funding for military housing and for military family support services. All this while there are a mere fifteen beds at Fort Benning for soldiers suffering from mental health issues, meaning that it takes ten months to get help if you are a soldier with a psychological issue. Somehow, though, we found room in the budget to set aside $20 million for a celebration when we win the wars in Afghanistan and Iraq.[25] This much bullshit can sink a battleship.

Five years into an undeclared War on Terror and we have not increased the size of the military and only recently started to talk about beefing up our overall strength. Any questions? These guys are not serious—not in the way of winning serious, not in a way anyone who wants to fight terrorism recognizes.

We are not willing to take even the smallest political risk that could help win this war, including telling the American people the truth. We don't do this because decisions are made by a bunch of stupid, mostly white men in suits who care more for their careers than they do for the defense of our country and the safety of our citizens.

Hell, half the time we don't even know whom we're fighting. The groups that claimed responsibility for the July 2005 bombings in London were groups we had never heard of until they struck. Every day new terror groups are popping up all over the world and we think we are in a "struggle"?

Al-Qaeda *knows* they are fighting a war and they are winning. They aren't winning in the conventional, World War II, treaty-signing way. They aren't winning in the invade-and-take-over-a-country kind of way, but they are winning the terrorism way. We should recognize this because we learned this very tough lesson forty years ago in the jungles of Vietnam.

They are winning because bin Laden is still alive. For over five years we have not been able to find a 6'4" Arab guy dragging a dialysis machine around the mountains of Pakistan. They are winning because just four weeks after the first attacks in London, bin Laden's right-hand man, Ayman al-Zawahiri, pointed his bony, blood-drenched finger at us and issued the threat of more attacks. This man threatened to kill us and our friends, and he is still breathing. That is a sure sign that the bad guys are winning. If this is going to continue, we might as well pack it in, find due east, bend over, and start praying in the direction of Mecca.

Since 9/11 we have had elections, wars, speeches, and suicide bombers in London, Madrid, and other places all over the world—some 6,000 terrorist attacks worldwide, in fact.[26] But we've had not a single real, we-are-sure-they-are-dead victory over terrorists. The terrorists are winning because we allow it, period. Iran has the bomb and is openly threatening Israel. Hamas, a terrorist organization, won an election and is running the Palestinian territory. Oh, and guess who supports Hamas? That would be Iran. While this is not exactly losing, it sure as hell is not winning. We allow it by lack of aggressive action; we allow it by our unwillingness to do the things that must be done.

Afghanistan looked great for a while, but the Taliban are back. And Iraq is, at best, a work in progress.

So what now? Now we get this figured out or we reap the whirlwind of defeat.

We get this right or we will be destroyed.

CHAPTER 3

THE PLAIN TRUTH ABOUT IRAQ

If how poorly prepared we are for the War on Terror scares you—and it should—then the war in Iraq should really make your hair stand on end. We have gone from a great victory in Iraq, in which we lost fewer than 160 of our great soldiers and marines, to an insurgency and then to a civil war in which we have had more than 23,000 men and women killed or wounded.

What the hell happened?

We attacked and kicked Saddam Hussein's ass because he supposedly had weapons of mass destruction (WMDs), was building nuclear weapons, and had barrels of chemical agents. We saw satellite pictures of trucks running around the desert with nasty stuff inside—except when we went in and looked for them, we found nothing. For two years, 1,500 experts ran around trying to find anything that even remotely looked, smelled, or tasted like a nuke, chemical weapon, or biological agent. At the end of this mad search, we were told the stuff ain't there—they don't know if it was ever there, and even if it was there, they have no idea where or when it went elsewhere.

At a time when our focus needed to be deadly accurate, we were distracted by bad intelligence gathered by incompetent people who were more concerned with politics than our safety. I've said this before and I will keep on saying it. To understand this is to understand the crux of the problem with the War on Terror and the war in Iraq. These are the same incompetent people who missed the warning signs of 9/11. It would have been impossible for these guys to screw up the intelligence on Iraq had they been fired after their first colossal blunder. But that didn't happen. Instead of standing in the unemployment line, they were at their desks using four-year-old questionable intelligence to justify sending us into a war where more than 24,000 Americans have been killed or wounded.

The president has said that Iraq is where the terrorists have decided to make their stand. He has said Iraq is the face on this War on Terror. Well, maybe it is now, but that's only because we made it that way. The truth is this: when we invaded Iraq, it was a bad place, but it was not an imminent threat. Iraq was not at the top of the list of the most dangerous terrorist nations.

Invading Iraq was, let's face it, a political act. But war should never be about political spin. For people like me, military action during the War on Terror is, and always will be, about terrorism and the well-being of Americans here and overseas.

Don't get me wrong, taking out Saddam was a good thing. He is a very bad guy who has finally been hanged, albeit poorly. I'm glad he's gone. I would have backed the war in Iraq if our government had said it was about influence in the Middle East, putting bases near Iran and Syria, and stopping Saddam from training terrorists at the secret Salman Pak facility. As the CIA and FBI have confirmed, this facility was a training enclave for terrorists right up until February 2003. We also know that the Iraqi regime gave $25,000 to each of the killers of Israel's children. But that wasn't the deal we bought. The deal was that Saddam was developing WMDs and we needed to stop him before he used them.

Sure, practically everyone conceded that Saddam had WMDs, Democrats included. Senator John Kerry got up before the Senate in October 2002 and said, "The threat of Saddam Hussein with weapons of mass destruction is real. . . . These weapons represent an unacceptable threat."[1] Hell, I admit that even I was wrong—totally, inexorably wrong. Numerous times on Fox News I said, "They had WMDs by the ton in Iraq." I had sources who were usually great and I listened to them. Some of these sources were in the Pentagon, and some were actually writing the papers for the White House.

We cannot and should not let ourselves—or the intelligence community—off the hook for being dead wrong about Iraq. There are only two possible explanations for what happened: either we *knew* that Saddam didn't have WMDs and people in power lied about it, or we *should have known* and our leaders are incompetent. Both explanations are totally unacceptable. When we're sending people overseas to die for us, incompetence and lies are unforgivable.

Now we have to face the truth. We need to state without reservation that we were *wrong*. Why? Iran is why. How can we even begin to talk about Iran and nukes and what needs to be done until we admit to, and fix, the things we got wrong in *Iraq*? We can't. We can't take action against Iran, or even talk about Iran, until we have some reason to have faith in our intelligence community, until we know we are better than we were, until we have at least a shot at getting this right.

"TURNED DOWN FLAT"

There have been lots of wrongs in this war.

It was never in question that the United States would win the wars in Afghanistan and Iraq; neither country had an army worth a damn. What was in question was how many soldiers we would need to keep the peace in both countries once the military victory was realized. And now it's crystal clear that the United States blew it on this question.

From the beginning, the government's mantra was that the generals responsible for Iraq would get what they needed. If the generals asked for more troops, then—*poof*—they would have them.

Uh, not really.

During the planning process leading up to the war in Iraq, the generals consistently asked for more troops and were turned down by Defense Secretary Donald "I-ask-and-answer-my-own-questions" Rumsfeld.

In a great book, *Cobra II,* Michael R. Gordon and Bernard E. Trainor show us that Rumsfeld controlled almost every aspect of the deployment to Iraq. He was in charge. He made the decisions. The buck stopped with him. Rumsfeld was presented with a workable plan, but he told the generals to tear it up and make one designed for a smaller force. He then rejected every other plan that was presented to him until the troop numbers were what he, and not the generals, wanted.

Why did he want a smaller force? Because that was in keeping with his vision for a new military, a leaner machine that went in, got the job done, and then left. He loved how the Special Forces, with the help of the CIA, took Afghanistan. So why not take Iraq the same way? Oh, I don't know, could it be because it was a different country and a different damned enemy?

The smart guys with experience knew we needed more troops to win and keep the peace, and they said so. They were told no. It wasn't just at the beginning of the war either. In fact, according to *Time* magazine, in August 2005 a senior military officer on the ground requested more troops and "got turned down flat."[2]

Here again we see how the blanket rejection of "nation building" can get us in big trouble. Yes, a smaller, lightning-quick force is a nice vision, but it is not appropriate for every situation. Sometimes, as in Iraq, more is needed. Yes, more—like a damn plan to win, a damn plan to put a government in place, a damn plan to seal the borders. Anything would've been better than what we got!

You may not want to do nation building, but what happens when, in taking a country, you severely damage its infrastructure? What happens if you haven't won the hearts and minds of the population? Are you safer then?

The truth is, whether we wanted to or not, we are doing nation building in both Afghanistan and Iraq, and both countries would be in better shape because of these efforts if almost anyone else had been secretary of defense. Hell, they would be in better shape if we'd had no one as secretary of defense.

Put bluntly, thousands of men and women have died because of the misguided, arrogant, and immensely stupid decision not to take the generals' recommendations.

But not all of the blame can be pinned on one person, or on the political leadership alone. Officers in the United States military are honor- and duty-bound to speak up if they believe a plan or action is wrong. If they speak up and still no one is listening to them, they are then duty-bound to resign. Once they resign, they can protest till the cows come home. They can go on TV and tell the American public what they know.

The problem with Iraq is that no one resigned in protest. No officer, in any service, quit over the issue of troop levels or any of the other mistakes we made. Officers are obligated to lead; they swear an oath to do so. Leading takes guts, something in short supply with those who left Rumsfeld's office with their balls cut off and went to war with a plan they knew was wrong. Taught from puberty to say "Yes, sir," "No, sir," and "Can do, sir," most U.S. officers have the mentality of "go along to get along."

This mind-set is killing us.

FAILED STRATEGIES

If not sending enough troops had been our only mistake, it would have been bad enough. But I am hard-pressed to name one strategic decision we made that *wasn't* a colossal mistake. Secretary of State Condoleezza Rice said she was sure we had made "thousands of tactical errors," but she was wrong; we made *strategic* errors.[3] Rice may have a doctorate, but she doesn't seem to know the difference between *strategic* and *tactical.* Look it up, Doc! Then rethink your "thousands of tactical mistakes" comment. You made a massive number of *strategic* mistakes.

Strategic refers to the big-picture stuff, such as attacking a country, deciding whom to put in as president, creating a spy network, moving a battle group off the coast of Iran, or even putting a submarine with cruise missiles off the coast of North Korea. In case you wanted to know, soldiers—hell, most officers—don't ever make strategic decisions (invade this country, bomb that one). Those decisions are held for the big boys: generals, mostly with four stars, as well as lots of elected and non-elected civilians who run the Department of Defense.

Tactical decisions, on the other hand, occur on the ground. Deciding to attack today with three units, which town to clear, which roadblock to put up, and which units to send into combat—these are all tactical decisions. Soldiers are the ones who make such decisions, and they make them in conditions that are similar to the ninth circle of hell.

When those in charge make their strategic decisions, they do so wrapped around how-will-this-look crap. Soldiers never do that. They tell you the truth, straight up, take it or leave it. How about we let soldiers make some of these strategic decisions? Hell, they are the ones paying for them.

Whenever people discuss why the fight in Iraq and Afghanistan isn't going well, there's a huge elephant in the living room they choose to ignore. It's this: *our military leaders have almost zero combat experience.* Because of this, they have never known what to do besides make more PowerPoint slides and protect their own asses. General John Abizaid, the MFFC (main motherfucker in charge), has two days of actual fighting in Grenada. General George Casey, the head guy in Iraq, has . . . hold on, let me count them . . . *zero* days in combat. So of course, the hard decisions—how to deploy snipers, whether to disband the Iraqi army and police, whether to pull out of Fallujah—were made by men who had no combat experience on which to base those decisions. There is at least one guy still around who has seen serious combat and is a four-star general. That man is Jim Jones, the NATO commander. He should have been in charge or at least have been the chairman of the Joint Chiefs of Staff. What happens when you let leaders without real combat experience make decisions? You get over 24,000 Americans killed or wounded. The soldiers pay the price, as they always have.

Time to throw the bullshit flag!

I meant it when I said that taking out Saddam was a good thing, but the Pentagon got everything else wrong. Even now, four years after the Army and Marine Corps did a great job taking Iraq, the Pentagon is still getting it wrong.

It took less than three weeks for our soldiers to get to Baghdad. Many of my great friends, soldiers with whom I served, were among the first into Iraq and Baghdad, and they have told me over and over that there was no plan for the peace. I have heard this from guys at all different levels and in all different services: generals, colonels, captains, sergeants, Navy SEALs, Special Forces soldiers, you name it. To a man, they say they weren't given a scintilla of guidance on what to do once they won the war. They never had any doubt that we would win, but none of them was told what to do the morning after.

We had brilliant scholars, military historians, military planners, the entire branch of Special Forces, and at least one television military analyst who were saying before the war that keeping the peace in Iraq was going to be eminently more difficult than the administration had predicted. But because of Rumsfeld's "vision" and the lack of balls on those in and out of uniform, we believed that the Iraqi people would welcome us as liberators. These were the people who thought controlling a population of 27 million would be easy. They also thought that the infrastructure would remain intact and that the country would have working electricity and water.

What were they drinking? What really happened is we *destroyed* a country and had to rebuild it from the ground up. For example, we have had to inoculate every child in Iraq and build more than three thousand schools. While that is a wonderful achievement by our guys, we could have done more, and done it quicker and easier, if we had *planned* for it.

Bottom line, when it came to Iraq we left out an essential ingredient: we failed to plan to win the peace. We didn't have the builders, the medical personnel, the jailers, or the other necessary workers ready to come in and help. Nor did we have the personnel to train the Iraqi people to help in the rebuilding. This failure has hurt and killed far too many of our finest people in uniform.

WEAKNESS

What did our guys in Iraq get instead of the things they really needed? They got Jay Garner.

Garner, a retired three-star Army general, was given the job to fix Iraq—specifically, as head of the Coalition Provisional Authority (CPA). But he was given no money, no staff, and no power. He began reconstruction efforts in March 2003 with plans to hold Iraqi elections within ninety days and to quickly pull U.S. troops out of the cities to a desert base. Garner should have known better than to take this or any job under those circumstances. The guy in charge *must* have control over the money and have tasking authority. Garner had neither; he also lacked the guts to tell Rumsfeld to stick it. Garner's can-do spirit and ego got in the way, and it had the predictable result—failure. He was replaced by L. Paul Bremer on May 11, 2003.

Bremer knew next to nothing about the job for which he had been chosen. He also hated the intelligence community, loathed the military, and had neither the experience nor dignity to be king. He also, like Garner before him, lacked the authority to be king. He had to ask permission to use the military through Rumsfeld. So not only was he not a king, mayor, or governor, he was worse—he was Rumsfeld's cabana boy.

We had about sixty days after we got to Baghdad to demonstrate that we were in charge. We should have established control. We knew how this should be done. We had done it in other countries. We had done it, at least partially, in Afghanistan, and we'd done it better in Bosnia and Kosovo. Yes, those operations were flawed, and for sure they were different, yet they had taught us how to do this kind of thing. We were successful in Bosnia—I know, because I was there. We had real leadership in the manner of one admiral "Snuffy" Smith. There had been three warring factions before we took over, and we had to overcome the United Nations' blundering disaster as a peacekeeping force.

Still, we managed to stop the war, and today we are almost out of there. The experience taught us a lot about how to win. Hell, we even wrote it down, and those of us who did it are still alive.

The same goes for Kosovo, where a peace deal is now in place and we have only a few U.S. troops. We had a plan there, we stuck to it, and we used the United Nations. We put Kosovo on the right track and we did it by doing all the things we are not doing in Iraq.

After we won on the ground in Iraq, we should have known that we needed to quickly find an Iraqi face to be head of the government. But instead of doing what we knew was necessary, we put Paul "It-ain't-my-fault" Bremer in charge. We have a series of historical lessons in victory and failure that come from World War II, Korea, Vietnam, and the Balkans, but we didn't bother to crack open this history book. We actually believed the political rhetoric that went against all the historical lessons learned. We believed that we would be welcomed as liberators instead of occupiers.

In his book, Bremer talks about how he initially recommended shooting the looters and instilling law and order, but when it leaked to the press, he backed down. Everyone was afraid of how it would look, so instead of shooting looters, Bremer, Rumsfeld, and General Abizaid had a conversation about the rules of engagement. Looters were not shot, order was not established, and the insurgency was born.

This is yet another example of where a bad decision has caused our men and women to die. When we didn't show strength in Iraq, it implied weakness. Terrorists feed on weakness. Years later we are still scrambling to right this and many other wrongs.

It has been suggested that if we had shot looters, CNN, Al Jazeera, or both would have condemned us and the Muslim world would have been aroused to anger. Could they have gotten more pissed off than flying planes into our buildings? I would have called Al Jazeera and announced that it was U.S. policy to shoot looters. Then I would have gone out, done it, and left the body in the street with a tag written in Arabic that read, "We shoot looters." The result would have been no more looting.

DUMB IDEA #1

Our next brilliant move was to disband the Iraqi army and the entire Iraqi police force. At the time of this brainless decision, we had 140,000 soldiers in country. That's 140,000 soldiers to control 27 million people. Can you imagine that briefing? *Yes, sir, we have 40,000 police in New York City for a population of a few million relatively law-abiding citizens. So why not 140,000 soldiers to control 27 million people in a population that is anything but law-abiding?* As a result of this faulty logic, looters raided buildings in Baghdad while our soldiers stood on a corner a block away.

Disbanding the army and police force could have been a fine decision only if a ready-made alternative army and police force were standing by. The new army and police would also have needed the same knowledge of the population and an ability to communicate in the language of the people. They would also have needed to be somewhat trained in police and military tactics. But we didn't have that at all. We had been victorious in defeating Saddam's forces, but we now occupied a country where almost everyone did not like us and we were surrounded by other countries that also did not like us and had open borders. Therefore, dismantling the Iraqi army and police was the number one dumb idea in a war that has seen a legion of dumb ideas. Some military Iraqi units had disappeared, but some had not. Some cops had run away, some had not. The looting did not help, but we had planned to deal with it by using the Iraq police and military until Bremer showed up, panicked, and signed a piece of paper dismissing them all. This yielded the predictable result—chaos.

SCREWED

So let's review. Not only did we not shoot looters, we disbanded the only law and order for 27 million people without having any replacements ready. Then we did not begin to train anyone to take their place for *six months*. Oh, and when we finally did begin to train some, we trained them as border guards instead of soldiers. When these border guards went to work, they ran away at the first sign of trouble.

If we had not disbanded the military and police, but instead had equipped them with radios and some advisers, monitored them, and taken appropriate action whenever and wherever necessary, they could have at least guarded the ammo dumps and streets while our skilled warriors did their jobs. It also would have put an Iraqi face on the operation, which would have made us look less like occupiers and more like liberators.

If we had shot a looter or two, allowed the event to be captured on television, and made sure the world saw it, the Iraqis and the whole world would have known that we really meant business. Instead, the message we sent to everyone was that we are bullies who are not willing to listen to anyone. We behaved like self-deceiving 800-pound gorillas with about as much brainpower as you would expect from the species. We were being foolish. Our friends in the Middle East shook their heads; those of us in the cheap seats screamed. We wanted to do this on the run—take a country and come home to a parade! We looked like a group of new guys who were not serious but were foolish and extremely incompetent.

Sooner or later we have to admit that what happened next was a proliferation of lies. Senators asked how it was going. Our Department of Defense said great—the Iraqi military training was on track. Then we watched 5,000 "trained" Iraqi police run away in Mosul. *Lie!* "The generals got what they asked for." *Big lie!* There is not an insurgency. *Huge lie!* The government that responded this way is not a government I recognize. Soldiers, avert your eyes; your leaders are not worthy of you.

General Tommy Franks saw there was going to be trouble and decided to take a victory lap and get the hell out of there. He left thirty days after we took Baghdad. He left when there was no plan on the table to implement the running of the country; no team was standing by; no Iraqi face like Hamid Karzai in Afghanistan was there to lead. We had nothing but Ahmed Chalabi of the so-called Iraqi National

Congress, but he caused a major pissing contest between the CIA and the departments of State and Defense. The CIA trusted him and the State Department did not, and all the while Chalabi was putting his own personal greed and self-importance before his own country.

Chalabi was a favorite source of such notable CIA greats as Dewey Claridge, the very talented and brave co-founder of the CIA's Counter Terrorism Center. Chalabi had, and still has, many supporters within our government. He also has powerful enemies. At the beginning of this war Chalabi was sent into Iraq on an American C-130 with 300 of his followers. But in May 2004, U.S. and Iraqi forces raided his home and office. There were allegations that Chalabi had passed sensitive U.S. intelligence to Iran. Ultimately any charges were dropped, and in fact Chalabi was eventually named a minister in the Iraqi government, where he wielded significant power. Someday they'll produce a made-for-TV movie about all of this called *How We Came to Love, Hate, Love, Then Just Tolerate Ahmed Chalabi While Turning Iraq into a Chaotic Mess.*

The truth is, what we got from this guy is what we should have expected—screwed. Sleeping with the devil gets you horns in the ass every time.

Those in charge decided that their own self-interest, or that of their agencies, was more important than the safety and security of the nation. They were concerned with reputations and/or promotions. They behaved disgracefully and should be told so . . . while they are being fired. As a result of all of this incompetence, we ran smack-dab into the middle of an insurgency and became blinded by our own arrogance. Very quickly the fat Muqtada al-Sadr filled the power vacuum *we* had created.

LOSING AL-SADR

When we invaded Iraq, Muqtada al-Sadr was a small-time, loud-mouthed cleric with no more than 200 armed men in his militia. Then we allowed him to become powerful. The following is the time line for the fiasco that created al-Sadr's rise to power[4]:

July 2003—In the newspaper *Al-Hawza,* Muqtada al-Sadr publishes an attack on Iraqis who are cooperating with the coalition forces. Listing 124 Iraqi "traitors" by name, he states that "hitting these people is a patriotic and religious duty." He also declares his intention to build an "Islamic Army" independent of the government.[5]

August—The CPA issues a warrant for al-Sadr for his direct involvement in the murder of Ayatollah Abd al-Majid al-Khoei, an influential moderate Shia who fought against the Baath party in 1991 and was forced to leave Iraq when the uprising was crushed. Al-Khoei had returned to Iraq shortly before his death to be the spiritual leader of the city of Najaf. Two eyewitnesses are prepared to testify that they heard al-Sadr give the order to kill al-Khoei, but on August 4, General Ricardo Sanchez, the new head of coalition forces in Iraq, says he needs "three or four days to make plans and position troops to backstop the Iraqi police" during the arrest.[6]

August—Marines stationed in Najaf actively campaign within the coalition military command to prevent al-Sadr's arrest. The Marines also lobby against his arrest at the Pentagon. This seems to be typical bureaucratic and military infighting. Bremer will later speculate that the opposition arises because the 1st Marine Expeditionary force is scheduled to rotate out of Iraq; no one wants to be the last Marine to die in Iraq. The next day, the CIA sends what Bremer calls a "near-hysterical" assessment of the risks involved in taking action against al-Sadr. The agency says that if we ignore him, he will go away.[7]

August 14—A U.S. helicopter accidentally knocks over a religious banner in Sadr City. In response, al-Sadr issues orders to rioters, calling it their "duty" to fire on Americans.[8]

August 15—CENTCOM commander General John Abizaid calls Bremer from Doha, Qatar, to express his concern about the plans to arrest al-Sadr—probably for fear of taking casualties and to avoid having to put down a Shiite uprising.[9]

August 18—Rumsfeld gives orders not to execute the plans to arrest al-Sadr.[10]

September—Al-Sadr declares the creation of an alternative Iraqi government, posing a direct challenge to the CPA's authority.[11]

October 7—Al-Sadr issues a fatwa that claims kidnapping is fine, and the occasional beheading too.[12]

October 10—Al-Sadr's "Mahdi Army" of 300 armed men attacks a U.S. patrol. Two U.S. soldiers are killed and others are wounded.[13]

October 12—Al-Sadr sets up illegal roadblocks in Najaf and Karbala. His followers take over mosques in Karbala. He stores ammunition and weapons in mosques.

General Abizaid reports that Deputy Defense Secretary Paul Wolfowitz is "going soft" on the most recent U.S. plan to arrest al-Sadr.

Al-Sadr's rebellion spreads. His army attacks the District Council government building and TV station. His troops occupy a police station, take over another mosque, and train youth in weapons and drill them in military formations near a shrine. He sets up a court to try Iraqis for offenses against Islam and announces that he does not recognize the authority of the CPA or the coalition military.

Gun battles in two holy cities go on for days while the United States tries to come up with a plan for dealing with al-Sadr.[14]

October 16—Al-Sadr's fighters kill three more Americans in Karbala. The unrest spreads into southern cities.

Bremer fires the Iraqi police chief and tells General Sanchez that the Americans have to take back the District Council building.

Local cops let an unknown number of al-Sadr's guys walk away from the building with their weapons.[15]

October 18—The 1st Armored Division moves on the Mahdi Army irregulars occupying Sadr City. They meet with little resistance.[16]

October 20—The operation in Karbala meets with no resistance and the fugitives are removed from the mosque. But al-Sadr is still at large.[17]

January 2004—Al-Sadr's forces kidnap four Iraqi policemen and march them into a mosque in Najaf. Al-Sadr's men announce their intention to have a sharia court—that is, a religious court to hand down Islamic law—to try the policemen and others they have kidnapped. After the trials, al-Sadr's forces put the kidnapped in a "secret prison."

Al-Sadr's militia has grown to 6,000 men from a mere 200. He makes known his intention to take power by force and calls for resistance against the coalition and the Governing Council of Iraq, which the CPA appointed in the summer of 2003.[18]

March 12—The Mahdi Army attacks a town near Najaf, knocking down houses, burning the ruins, and dragging off eighteen men to al-Sadr's prison, where they will be tortured. Several dozen women and children from the town go missing.[19]

March 14—Bremer asks General Sanchez to round up some of al-Sadr's guys. Sanchez says, "We'll work on it, sir."[20]

March 23—Well-armed members of al-Sadr's Mahdi Army take over the Kufa mosque.[21]

March 24—Al-Sadr's army, broadly engaged across the south, continues kidnapping and torturing Iraqi policemen, and also sets up roadblocks.[22]

March 26—Al-Sadr's forces attack the CPA-sponsored democracy centers in several southern cities and get into a firefight with coalition troops.

In a speech, al-Sadr rants, "No! No! to Jews. No! No! to Israel! No! No! to America." He then praises the 9/11 terrorist attacks as "a miracle and blessing from God."

Bremer asks General Sanchez to come up with a plan to control al-Sadr's militia in the south.[23]

April 4—In several cities, al-Sadr's followers flood the streets around police stations and CPA offices. They attack the CPA compound in Najaf, killing one U.S. soldier and wounding several others. The compound looks like it could fall to the insurgents. Meanwhile, al-Sadr's troops begin attacking coalition offices in Karbala, Amara, Nasiriyah, and Al-Hillah.

An ambush in Sadr City results in the deaths of three Americans.

Al-Sadr issues a fatwa calling on the coalition to release all prisoners and on the Iraqis to force the coalition to leave Iraq.[24]

April 6—Coalition air strikes begin against al-Sadr's army in Sadr City.[25]

April 8—Al-Sadr's men overrun the coalition compound in Al-Kut.[26]

Our abysmal handling of this murderous, arrogant, and ignorant leader of an illegal militia in Iraq tells the story of our incompetence and our total lack of courage and leadership. It really tells little about al-Sadr—the fat bastard with a beard. He threatened us. He killed Americans. We said we were going to arrest him and we backed down. The most powerful nation on the planet was forced to back down. By allowing this to happen, we made him a hero. Care to guess how big his militia is now? It is more than 60,000 strong, and al-Sadr controls thirty seats in the new Iraqi parliament. Al-Sadr's power has grown every day. He is being supplied with money by Iran, and his power extends all the way from Baghdad to Basra, north to Mosul, and west to Ramadi. Large numbers of the death squads were recruited from his militia. He should be dead, but instead he is a major player in Iraq. All this because of our incompetence.

After Paul Bremer left unceremoniously from Iraq (leaving behind rampant corruption and no security in one-third of the country), he wrote a book and collected his keep-this-between-us Medal of Freedom. Also, not surprisingly, he has attempted to distance himself from any real mistakes in Iraq, including the al-Sadr debacle. But be clear: he owns part of this one, and American luminaries such as Paul Wolfowitz must take some blame as well, since they backed down also. General John "I-speak-Arabic-and-you-don't" Abizaid said not to kill al-Sadr. Marine Corps officers were lobbying against killing al-Sadr. The CIA told us if we ignored al-Sadr, he'd go away. Yeah, he went away all right. He went to a seat of power in the new government.

Not to kill this guy was the ultimate in spineless decisions. Ultimately, that decision fell to the secretary of defense. Yup, Rumsfeld again. Rumsfeld rejected the plan to go after al-Sadr because taking that action would pose a risk to his vision. He wanted no casualties, and dealing with militias was not part of the vision he had for this force. He wanted them in and out and to let this stuff be dealt with by the new government.

The failure to get al-Sadr sent a terrible signal to all: we allowed a murderer not only to walk but also to manipulate events to achieve power. And now he controls a militia the size of four U.S. Army infantry divisions. We have bodies in ditches with al-Sadr's fingerprints all over them. He has ordered killings; he has taken over entire neighborhoods; he is one of the major reasons Iraq has gotten bogged down in a civil war.

This all happened because those in and out of uniform failed. They failed to be tough. They blinked. They failed to protect our soldiers and Marines, and in so doing, they failed to protect our country.

CIVIL WAR

I know what some of you are thinking: *Civil war? Did he really say civil war?* Yeah, I did. There's been endless bickering about whether Iraq has descended into a civil war or whether it is simply dealing with sectarian violence. Sectarian violence? Is that what you call it when half the population is fighting the other half? By late 2006 the Iraqi population was losing more than 100 a day to this "sectarian violence."

There have been thousands of Iraqi civilians, with their hands tied behind their backs and hoods over their heads, shot and killed and their bodies dumped all over Iraq. The Iraqi government can't stop it, the U.S. military isn't being allowed to stop it, and so it's growing. This is a civil war.

In my opinion Iraq has been in a civil war for a while now. The civil war started the day they blew up the Golden Mosque. But the politicians have said, "No, Iraq is not in a civil war." The logic they have used to justify not calling it a civil war is that the sectarian violence has not been aimed at the government, it has just been two sides fighting each other. Well, if their definition were true, and I don't think it is, then on October 15, 2006, Iraq officially began its civil war when a group of Sunni insurgents declared that they were starting their own government—a separate Islamic Republic of Iraq.[27] The carnage is so bad that the prime minister of Iraq, Nouri al-Maliki, has actually asked the president of Iran for help.[28] So 24,000 American men and women have been killed or wounded in Iraq to enable Iran to help with security and to gain further influence in Iraq? My God, I hope not.

The Shia and the Sunnis in Iraq are in a continuous dance of death, and the only thing keeping them apart at all, and not that well, is the good old USA.

This "sectarian violence" gathered steam just as a free, yet totally corrupt, Iraqi central government was trying to get its act together. This central government can't protect its own people, and neither, it appears, can the United States of America. For as much as we have tried, and with as much blood as we have spilled—and make no mistake, we have spilled gallons—we have been unable to stop the violence within Iraq. We have mosques being blown up and hundreds of Iraqi civilians being killed by roving death squads. Some of these death squads actually work for corrupt government agencies, while other members just dress as if they do. They are filling up the morgues in and around Baghdad. Iraqi civilians and American soldiers are still dying in unacceptable numbers. The "sectarian violence" rages, refugees have doubled, and the Sunnis and Shia are moving out of their mixed ethnic neighborhoods and are forming ghettos or leaving the country.

Call it what you want, but the facts don't change: it's a civil war.

Here is how it should have worked. When we first arrived, no one, and I mean no one, should have been allowed to put up a roadblock unless it was us. If anyone did this, we should have torn it down or shot those who erected it. Al-Sadr openly defied us, and instead of dying he got to live and prosper. If this is allowed, more al-Sadrs, more unrest, more bad things, and more dead Americans will be the result. In other words, you have failure.

The al-Sadr episode and our total lack of leadership and guts will be a main chapter in the "we fucked up in Iraq" book and movie if it finally all goes to hell. If we are lucky—and now, unfortunately, we need a lot of luck to turn this around—and the good guys prevail, then we are doomed to repeat this mistake. The mistake is simple: bad guys should never kill us and be allowed to live; they must die, horribly and immediately. If we made the correct tactical decision here, it would have given pause to the next bad guy. At least it would have given us practice in killing the next bad guy if he committed the same folly.

TWO STEPS FORWARD, THREE STEPS BACK

In this war, we take two steps forward and then three back. In May 2005 a British helicopter was shot down, killing five brave British soldiers. How did the citizens of the town of Basra react? How did al-Sadr's illegal militia react? They threw firebombs and stones at the helicopter and the soldiers trying to rescue those inside. Basra was supposed to be calm; the British were supposed to be in charge there.

Abu Ghraib continues to be the most embarrassing moment for the United States in Iraq. The prison was a symbol of all that was wrong with Saddam. It should have been blown up and never used again, but no, we used it, and soldiers and their leaders lost their discipline and common sense in doing so. More than sixty front-page *New York Times* stories later, we are still using the place that Saddam used to torture his citizens. Abu Ghraib will forever be a symbol of two terrible things: first, it was Saddam's prison of torture, and second, it was the United States' prison of torture. While the latter is a stretch, at least half of this country and millions of Muslims believe it, which makes it something we have to constantly overcome. To the Muslim world we are being associated with torture because of the illegal actions of a few soldiers and the incompetence of a group of leaders starting with General Ricardo Sanchez.

We go into terrorist strongholds, clean up the place, and move on. We leave Iraqis behind to maintain the city, but they run away. So we have to go back in and do it again. We have taken Fallujah, Tall Afar, and countless other places again and again and again. Two steps forward, three steps back. Not a great showing of our military tactics, competence, or determination to fight the War on Terror.

Recently, at a graduation ceremony for the Iraqi military, the newly commissioned soldiers were told that they would be sent to Fallujah and not their hometown. The soldiers responded by resigning and stripping off their uniforms right there on the parade grounds.[29] Two steps forward, how many back?

Guess what? Our soldiers are dying. They are getting blown up, saving lives, rebuilding, giving freedom to a people who have never known it, and counting the days until they can come home. These are our best, our bravest; there are none better anywhere. Sadly, their bravery is not enough. With a policy that is bankrupt and led by inept leaders, our soldiers' bravery and competency are not enough. More than

24,000 have given their lives or parts of their bodies to this cause. If only for them, we should have gotten Iraq right. Instead, we keep losing more soldiers, and still the idiots on U.S. television and radio are yelling that things are going better.

In October 2006, one of these experts said, "The insurgency is over." This clown was a former general. Nice! This same historian/ political officer, who has forgotten that he was once a soldier, then said the airport road in Baghdad was safe, and today as I write this, we have just lost another fourteen people over there. In order for him to make such ridiculous statements, the general must have forgotten what it was like to be in combat. Being attacked more than 500 times a week is not a good thing, and saying it loudly on TV does not make it so.

We are still in the middle of a deadly insurgency in which terrorists put bombs in dead cows and dogs. The most powerful nation on the planet is getting its soldiers blown apart at an alarming rate. While we have not lost yet, we are certainly not winning. In an insurgency, that is just like losing.

We were going to make Iraq better. In 2005, 500 Iraqi civilians died each week because of violence. In September 2006, more than 3,500 Iraqis were killed.[30] The carnage continues unabated, averaging 150 a day. Oil production is down rather than up. The lights are still not on, and at least one-third of the country is in a civil war. Saddam is gone, but only the most avid advocate for what we did can say that the situation in Iraq is much better. At best, Iraq is a work in progress. My God, in the first three years of this war more than 50,000 Iraqi civilians were murdered and more than 24,000 Americans were killed or wounded. Our soldiers gave us a great military victory and our leaders pissed it away.

FIXING THIS MESS

We have a small window of opportunity left in Iraq to right the sinking ship before the politicians make it completely unworkable. Avoiding disaster is the first and most important step, but I also hope we don't accept that the thousands of soldiers killed or wounded gave their all for *workable.*

So what do we do?

Well, for starters, we need to send 1,000 more trainers to Iraq to get the police force into shape. Do you remember the first guy who "trained" the Iraq police? It was Bernie Kerik, a former New York City police commissioner. In June 2006 he pleaded guilty to accepting illegal gifts from a construction company with alleged mob ties; he was arrested, and paid a steep fine. This is the guy we chose to train the new Iraq police department. Any questions why that program didn't start out too well?

We can't have corrupt officials overseeing Iraq, where approximately $8 billion of our money is listed as missing and/or unaccounted for. We pay companies huge sums of money to turn on the water, get the oil flowing, make the lights work, and get the toilets to flush. How about we make sure they actually do it?

We need to beg Middle Eastern countries like Jordan and Saudi Arabia to step up and help us with soldiers and political support inside Iraq.

We need to announce to the world that we are withdrawing in six months and leaving 50,000 troops in three bases. Divide Iraq into thirds and let the Shia keep one section, the Sunnis take another, and the Kurds keep the north. Will giving the Kurds territory piss off the Turks? You bet—but they deserve it for not allowing us to use the northern approach from Turkey during the initial invasion in March 2003, and also for their persecution of the Kurds for decades. Put a U.S. military base in each third to continue influencing and watching Iraq, Syria, and Iran. This will help us finish the job we started—that is, to achieve a stable and secure Iraq. We should ensure that there is power sharing within a centrally located Iraqi government and that oil revenues are shared.

We have to leave Iraq stronger than it is right now, or the Iranians, Syrians, Russians, or Chinese will be all over it. We have done good stuff there and we need to notify the world that we are leaving Iraq stronger and in the capable hands of compassionate and competent leadership. We also need to be totally honest and admit to our mistakes.

I am suggesting we do the commonsense thing, the right thing. Don't just declare victory for political purposes, or pull out entirely and move on to the next place. Yes, we need to leave Iraq, but we need to leave it with enough support so that it doesn't collapse. And when we have done this, we need to show our appreciation for Americans in uniform by giving them a huge pay increase, a parade, and the universal thanks of a grateful nation.

Ask yourself some questions: Did the U.S. invasion of Iraq make us safer or better? Are the dead and wounded American soldiers worth what we are seeing in Iraq today? The answers to these questions are not reassuring, for while Iraq is definitely better off, America isn't.

CHAPTER 4

THE THREATS WE FACE

Suicide bombers came to the West on July 7, 2005. They pulled off a simultaneous, well-coordinated attack in London, and they did it while the eight leaders of the free world were meeting less than 500 miles away in Glasgow, Scotland. Three explosions went off at 8:50 A.M. and tore through three underground trains, leaving death and destruction in their wake. Emergency personnel rushed to the scene. Fifty-seven minutes later, the top of a double-decker bus was blown off and body parts were left in the road. When it was all over, 700 people were injured and 56 were dead, including the four suicide bombers.

The leaders of the United States, the United Kingdom, Canada, France, Germany, Italy, Japan, and Russia—the so-called Group of Eight, or G8—were gathered in Glasgow for their annual economic and political summit. The main item on the agenda? Climate change. So less than four years after 9/11, the main item on the agenda of a meeting of the world's most powerful leaders was climate change—not terrorism, but climate change.

The G8 conference had been scheduled for eighteen months. Before any meeting like this takes place, the national intelligence services of the eight biggest, richest, smartest, and most technologically savvy countries gear up. All technical and human intelligence assets had been fine-tuned and directed toward Glasgow and the surrounding area—including London. You know what that means? According to every single one of the world's billion-dollar-funded, best-and-brightest intelligence agencies, everything was fine.

Then, *bang*! Everything was not fine. The world's best and brightest totally missed it—again.

I ask you, how safe are you feeling now?

On July 21, two weeks to the day after the bombings, four Muslim men boarded three trains and a bus in London and tried to set off bombs. This time London was lucky. The terrorists screwed up and the bombs didn't explode. What happened next was the largest look-we-captured-the-bad-guys-*after*-they-tried-to-kill-us manhunt in British history. Two days later, July 23, three bombs went off simultaneously in a resort area in Egypt; the first was a planted bomb, and the second and third were suicide car bombs. Eighty-three people were killed.

The questions blared from every television set: Are the attacks related? Could the United States be next?

Could we be next? Are suicide bombers on their way to the United States? Not only could it happen, but it will happen if we don't begin to really understand what we are facing. Unless you've been living under a rock, you know that in August 2006, a terrorist plot was uncovered to simultaneously blow up planes traveling from Great Britain to the United States. The result of this was three hours at the gate instead of one, no carry-on bags allowed, no carry-on liquids of any kind. Here we go again! We are one step away from flying naked. The truly disturbing thing is that so long as we're looking for the bomb and not the bomber, so long as we're trying to detect the method of death rather than using intelligence to stop those who plan to employ that method, we are losing the War on Terror and we are less safe than we should be.

I'm glad we caught the bad guys. Great work! The good guys won this one. But everyone who looked at this should know that the bad guys are still there and still plotting—still coming up with ingenious ways to kill us.

TARGET: AMERICA

The worldwide jihad is expanding. It is now using citizens of civilized countries, those who enjoy every freedom, and they are being used against the very countries that give them their freedom. The suicide bombers who accomplished their task and killed fifty-two people in the London subways were British citizens. All but one were born and raised in England. They had families and wives. Two of them had children. One of them left behind a pregnant wife. Their parents expressed surprise; their friends and neighbors said they were good people. No one suspected them.

Similarly, the terrorists arrested for the failed July 23, 2005, bombings were a group of immigrants who came to England as children and were given permission to stay. Their potential victims were guilty of giving their would-be assassins clothing, housing, education, training, doctoring, and legal counsel.

Then there were the people arrested in 2006 in connection with the massive terrorist plot to blow up airliners. Of the nineteen arrested, many were born in Britain, and all of them were raised there.[1]

Get the picture? The terrorists use the very freedoms given to them to kill their benefactors.

This kind of thing could easily happen here. *Especially* here. Nowhere do citizens and visitors enjoy more freedoms than in the United States. That makes our country great, but it also makes us vulnerable to attack.

Even if the terrorists aren't homegrown, we can be certain that they are plotting to attack us again. If you need a reminder of that, look no further than the London airliner plot that was broken up in 2006. It's a question of *if*, not *when*. In fact, according to a broad-ranging survey of arms experts conducted in 2005 by the chairman of the Senate Foreign Relations Committee, there is a 50 percent chance a biological, chemical, or radiological attack will strike somewhere in the world in the next five years. Over the next ten years, these experts concluded, the chances of attack jump to 70 percent.[2]

How safe are you feeling now?

MUSHROOMING THREATS

According to the arms experts surveyed by the Senate, the most likely major weapon to be used is a radiological weapon, or dirty bomb. And you can bet your ass the terrorists are trying to get their hands on radioactive material. Lieutenant Colonel Robert L. Domenici (U.S. Army, Ret.) is the COO of Strategic Response Initiatives and an expert in the area of emergency preparedness, counterterrorism, and disaster management, especially involving weapons of mass destruction. If anyone knows about dirty bombs, it's Domenici. And what he told me isn't encouraging.

When asked how we stop bad guys from obtaining radioactive materials, he said, "I am not sure we can stop someone from obtaining radioactive material or bomb-making material if they want to get it. There are just too many ways to obtain it, just like chemical and biological agents." Domenici is right. In the former Soviet bloc nations especially, they're having a tough time securing their uranium, plutonium, and other radioactive resources.

And of course, we can't rule out the threat of nuclear attack. It's bad enough that madmen like North Korea's Kim Jong-il and Iran's Mahmoud Ahmadinejad have nuclear weapons programs and that, as the arms experts surveyed by the Senate concluded, up to five more countries could acquire nuclear weapons in the next decade.[3] Even worse, the terrorists are desperate to get their hands on the bomb too. But don't take my word for it. Just read what Osama bin Laden's manual for his followers says: "This is a duty on the Muslims to possess a nuclear bomb."

We need to get a handle on all this stuff. We need to force other countries not only to secure their radiological waste but also to secure and destroy their nukes. The biggest problem is that loose nukes are floating around Russia. Sure, some people suggest that there are no loose nukes or suitcase nukes. Well, they have never been to Russia or delved into the well-documented intelligence gathered by the U. S. Special Forces. If they had, they would know three things: the Russians have almost no controls on their nukes, there is no Russian nuke that cannot be bought, and there are nukes that fit in a large suitcase.

Currently, we have a long-term plan in place to secure Russia's loose nukes, but it is screwed up. Besides, we need solutions *now,* not in the long term. The so-called Nunn-Lugar program began in 1991, authorizing $400 million a year of Defense Department funds to be spent to assist Russia in "the transportation, storage, safeguarding, and destruction of nuclear and other weapons" of the former Soviet Union and "to assist in the prevention of weapons proliferation." After initial problems were sorted out, the program seemed on track. But then the government cut the funding. The good news is that our government moved up the timetable for completion to 2008. That's a little better, but we're still not safe.[4] While we are waiting for the incredibly corrupt Russian government to get around to maybe getting serious about this problem, we could just buy the damn things from them and destroy them ourselves.

Domenici endorses the idea of buying loose nukes and bringing them back here to destroy: "Anytime you can disarm a former adversary that cannot control its borders both internally or externally, it is a good idea to get their nuclear weapons out of their hands and into ours. Otherwise, they will wind up in the wrong hands or causing a crisis at some point." As Domenici puts it, "money talks and nations walk to this beat." He says the United States "can speed up the process through trade, effecting critical relationships through technology transfers that will allow the host nation to take care of the problem internally."

The nuclear threat is so severe because it is so wide-ranging. We already know for sure that the terrorists have U.S. nuclear power plants in their sights. U.S. forces who moved into Afghanistan in 2001 found drawings of U.S. nuclear plants in al-Qaeda caves. After that, the nuclear industry spent a billion dollars beefing up security. Part of the new security specifications included running drills of mock terrorist attacks. Only one problem: the company they paid to do the drills was the same company that provided security to half of our nuclear power plants.[5] No conflict of interest there! This same company had to remove guards from a Florida plant in the spring of 2004 after they faked foot patrols. This same company once found two guards asleep and a gate open at a New Jersey plant. This same company discovered guards had cheated during a mock terror drill at another government nuclear facility.[6]

Domenici reveals that an attack on one of our nuclear facilities could cause a meltdown. "A meltdown could cause a plume of radioactive material to be carried downrange and affect a large land mass. . . . The effects from the plume of radioactive substances that were dispersed downrange would be long range. An increase in cancer rates as well as other ailments would be ongoing for many years to decades."

And then, as Domenici said, there are the biological agents that we need to worry about. A biological attack on the United States could be deadly. Of course, we've already had a biological attack on our country. What, you don't remember? Just after 9/11, someone, or a group of someones, attacked us using anthrax. Five people died, thirteen others suffered anthrax infections, and yet again, our nation's Capitol was shut down for a day.

Do you remember how those cases were adjudicated? No? Allow me to assist. No culprits were found; no one was arrested; nothing was traced to anyone or any country. The one guy we thought might have done it sued the government for making him a "person of interest." Some five years later, no one has been arrested and the task force investigating the incident is hardly holding any meetings. They have turned to other matters.

This was not some super-secret bomb or sophisticated device. These attacks were carried out by mailing letters through our own postal system. This was death delivered by inserting a small amount of poisoned powder in an envelope. Was it a homegrown nut? A terrorist group? We don't know. Maybe it was a test run. Maybe next time they will do it better.

We need to make sure we are doing everything we can, here and abroad, to secure biological and chemical agents that, with the right expertise, could become weapons. This does not include mistakenly sending deadly influenza virus to other countries, which our own Centers for Disease Control did in April 2005. Millions of dollars supposedly spent on bioterrorism preparedness and this is what we get? It's ridiculous and we need to stop it now.

Seriously, how safe are you feeling now?

VULNERABILITIES

America's nuclear power plants aren't the only target for terrorists. No way. There are plenty of other targets—targets that we make easier to hit because we're doing a terrible job securing them. Take our vast network of train tracks that go in and around cities like New York, Boston, Los Angeles, and Denver. These cities have literally thousands of miles of totally unprotected tracks. The transformers and stations in all these cities are also unprotected. Our politicians have told us we are at war, so what is up with our trains? Nothing is up. We are very good at protecting, or at least looking like we are protecting, our airports, but we aren't even pretending to protect our rail transportation infrastructure.

That's true not just in the big cities but across the country. There are hundreds of thousands of miles of railroad across the United States and almost none of it is protected. Very little of it is fenced, and closed-circuit TV monitoring is used only minimally. Twenty years ago we had 4,000 railroad police officers who protected our trains twenty-four hours a day, seven days a week. Today, we have only 1,300 railroad police officers sworn to protect our rail system.

That's right—even after being attacked on our own soil, and after witnessing suicide bombers attacking trains in London and Madrid, we have actually continued to reduce the forces that could prevent a terrorist attack. The Association of American Railroads and the individual

Class I railroads claim to be doing many proactive things such as beefing up patrols and participating in various Homeland Security committees and planning cells. But where the metal meets the track, they have done little.

With the reduced staff, the railroads have completely reorganized their security system. The organizations that employed the security officers used to be run like municipal police departments, meaning that the officers regularly patrolled a specific area and so, like beat cops, they knew how the place ran. But today, one special agent is assigned to cover a large territory—anywhere from 200 to 700 miles of railroad. These agents work nine to five and are on call to respond to incidents as needed. What does this mean? It means there's very little security during the day, and on nights and weekends no one is watching the railroads. When the security officers were local, the response rate was almost immediate and there was a familiarity with the local terrain.

But don't fret; it is not hopeless. We have experts like Kevin Lynch, a railroad police practices consultant. Lynch has been a captain in the Consolidated Rail Corporation (Conrail) Police Department, a staff captain in the Conrail Police System Headquarters (which controls Conrail Police in sixteen states and two Canadian provinces), and the Conrail division commander at Selkirk, New York, and the Bronx, New York. He knows how to fix this security problem. He prescribes simple target hardening—that is, strengthening the defenses of a site to deter the attack—and the lavish use of technology to act as force multipliers for the railroad police. How this translates is that we need good fencing, effective lighting, perimeter clearing, use of drone aircraft for track patrols, closed-circuit television, intrusion detection equipment, monitoring of dangerous or high-value cargo being shipped by rail, hazardous materials monitoring, alarms on all switches and signals, a much larger railroad police force so that all major rail yards and all main lines can be patrolled by uniformed railroad police 24/7, and the abolition of the special agent system and a return to a municipal police model.[7]

All these things can help. It will be expensive to do, sure, and it will take at least five years to get the various railroad police departments back up to where they once were. Even that wouldn't be enough, since we need to improve beyond where we were twenty years ago. But we need to start moving in the right direction, immediately. We've had five years since 9/11 and yet we haven't taken a single step in this direction.

Given that the railroad infrastructure is totally open, it won't take a bomb or a rocket-propelled grenade (RPG) to break a switch lock—all you need is a sledgehammer. Five or six sledgehammers simultaneously breaking five or six switch locks in various cities across a region or the entire United States could create a disaster of mass proportion, especially since freight trains move hazardous materials throughout our country. We're talking mass casualties and mass dislocations.

We can remedy our vulnerability if we just listen to the experts and make the case to the American people that spending some money can make us safer. Or we can wait for the next attack, or watch videos of the London and Madrid attacks and think, like we did for forty years before 9/11, it can't happen here.

How did that work for us?

Another area of vulnerability is our drinking water. In September 2004 the U.S. Government Accountability Office's director of natural resources and environment reported to Congress on the extent of the danger. He testified, "Drinking water utilities across the country have long been recognized as potentially vulnerable to terrorist attacks of various types, including physical disruption, bioterrorism, chemical contamination, and cyber attack. Damage or destruction by terrorists could disrupt not only the availability of safe drinking water, but also the delivery of vital services that depend on these water supplies, such as fire suppression. Such concerns were greatly amplified by the September 11, 2001, attacks on the World Trade Center and the Pentagon and then by the discovery of training manuals in Afghanistan detailing how terrorist trainees could support attacks on drinking water systems."[8]

Gotta love the language that government bureaucrats use. *Such concerns were greatly amplified* . . . You're damn right they were! You know what those terrorist manuals actually say? They lay out exactly how to poison our water supplies, not to mention other fun things like how to blow up bridges. The manuals are chilling in how matter-of-fact they are about killing innocents. So yeah, I'd say that our concerns should be "greatly amplified" at this point. In fact, go back and reread the previous paragraph, but this time translate the bureaucratese into plain English. Bioterrorist attacks, chemical warfare, no safe drinking water, no water available to put out fires (think the terrorists might find a way to take advantage of that vulnerability?). The threat couldn't be spelled out more clearly. This is a serious problem—deadly serious.

Even before the GAO official went before Congress, the government had made a show of addressing the problem. In 2002 Congress passed the Public Health Security and Bioterrorism Preparedness and Response Act, which was supposed to improve this nation's ability to prevent, prepare for, and respond to bioterrorism and other health emergencies. The act specifically addressed the drinking water issue, and Congress appropriated more than $140 million to help drinking water facilities improve security and reduce vulnerability.

But have we actually secured our drinking water? Not really. In fact, the government has done little to improve the security around this vital element in our nation's infrastructure. Most of the money was spent on studying the problem and coming up with some plans, but we didn't do any real fixing. Then, in May 2006, Congress proposed new legislation to deal with our drinking water vulnerability—but gee, isn't that what the 2002 act was supposed to do? This time, the legislation would require the Environmental Protection Agency and the Department of Homeland Security to reduce the risk of a terrorist attack using toxic chemicals. And where would the terrorists get those toxic chemicals? Why, from our very own drinking water facilities, which stockpile the chemicals for use in water treatment.

These dangerous chemicals need to be secured. Don't think this is a big deal? Try this on for size. According to the Homeland Security

Council, an explosion set off next to a chlorine gas tank could kill 17,500 people and send 100,000 others to the hospital.[9] Safer alternative chemicals are available, but it will take another $625 million to convert our facilities to these safer chemical treatments.

Now think for a minute about how dependent we are on computers. Can you say vulnerability? Terrorists with a computer and an Internet connection can take control of, or shut down, the Internet or our phone system—and then what? How about if they screw with the electrical system? In November 2001, computer hacker Vitek Boden was sentenced to two years in prison for using the Internet, a wireless radio, and stolen control software to release up to 1 million liters of sewage into the river and coastal waters of Maroochydore in Queensland, Australia.[10] Next time, instead of sewage, maybe it will be something worse.

Really, how safe are you feeling now?

THE ISLAMO-FASCIST THREAT

Of all the threats we face, the hardest to understand and combat is Islamo-fascism. While the Muslim faith is a noble religion, Islamo-fascism is the lethal and violent emanation of a convoluted form of that same religion. It is terrorism disguised as religion, and the religious aspect of this war makes combating it very difficult. The reasons for a holy war are usually not political or territorial; they are usually over a passage in the Koran or Bible. Sometimes they are over some unspoken offense that the nut jobs use to work themselves into a frenzy and build up the courage to come after us.

Twenty percent of the world's population practices some form of Islam, and it is estimated that millions of Muslims don't look kindly on the old US of A. As in any faith, extremists make a bigger splash than moderates; witness the case with al-Qaeda and Wahhabists. Wahhabism is the most virulent strain of Islam and the state religion of Saudi Arabia. The trouble with these extremists is that they make their splash with bombs, death, and destruction. They frighten the more moderate voices of the faith into silence. Silence does not help combat Islamo-fascism, and it therefore becomes de facto support.

This war is not a Christian crusade, but you need to make no mistake, it is a holy war—at least from the perspective of the terrorists. We are at war with Islamo-fascists and they are at war with us. They are the people who have declared this war for their own twisted reasons. We damned well need to pay attention to it and them, and then we need to figure out why it matters.

Just because the terrorists are religious nut jobs doesn't mean they are incompetent in the art of war. Killing does not take brilliance. These guys have been doing it for years, and they have been getting away with it. They are good at it, and when we allow them to get away with it without demonstrating the full force and fury of the U.S. military, it looks like they are winning.

We didn't declare this holy war, but we can and must win it. While we are killing as many terrorists as we can, we must also do some tree hugging or its religious equivalent. We need to engage in a long-term public relations campaign with the Muslim world. We need to bring the Muslim world more food, medicine, and machinery. We need to export business to these areas in order to provide economic opportunities. We need people on the ground demonstrating American charity and largesse. We need to export the good things America has and represents. We need to go to the mosques, the less fanatical madrassas (schools that teach the Koran and Muslim societal law), and the villages and cities where the moderate Muslims live, and win their hearts and minds. We need to give them a reason to work with us and against the Islamo-fascists.

TAKING UP THE FIGHT—FINALLY

There's one more threat we face—one of the greatest threats—and it's one all of us can do our part to eliminate. That threat is our own apathy.

Let's face it, we don't seem to care anymore. The images of 9/11 are long gone from the American psyche. These pictures have taken their place next to the grainy images of the beaches of Normandy, Pearl Harbor, and our military crawling through the jungles of Vietnam. For us, they are historical items to be dragged out on anniversaries and then quickly put away. This is a mistake. We think that because there hasn't been a recent attack on us, we are safer. It isn't true! We are more at risk now than we ever were. We need to care. And we need to speak out; it's the only way to ensure that our leaders hear us and make the changes necessary for our safety.

Apathy, like terrorism, is insidious. It creeps up on you. One day you are trying to find a parking spot at the mall and you drive into the only one you can find—except it is a handicapped spot. You say to yourself, "It's just for a minute" or "Just this one time." That is apathy talking. Apathy causes you not to care about other people. It allows you not to pick up the trash at your feet, not to call your neighbors when they are sick, or not to find a way to make it right with those you love. Apathy makes us stupid, wrong, and probably bound for hell.

Apathy feeds and enables terrorism. It allows us to look the other way. While we are looking the other way, men in caves, who are not apathetic, work toward one thing—our destruction.

It takes strong, persuasive, brave, and consistent leadership to overcome apathy. After 9/11, when people stood in line for hours to give blood and sent so many things to the rescue workers in New York that they had to be asked to stop, our leaders had an opportunity to bring the American people together. They had an opportunity to tell us the truth and to ask us to make sacrifices. They should have said, "This is a damn war!" They should have told us that winning would take sacrifice and hard work on the part of everyone. They should have told us what to expect: this war was going to hurt, this war was going to take a long time, and that in order to win it we will need everyone to help and contribute. But instead we were told to "go about our lives," that it should be business as usual. This was the wrong call because it fostered apathy.

The media have aided this indifference. Think back to July 2005 and the London bombings. They were all over the news for a couple of days, sure. But then the media quickly shifted back to the big news of the day—a blond girl who had gone missing from Aruba. What happened to the War on Terror?

Even when we debate important issues like the appointment of Supreme Court justices, the conversation centers on the candidates' views on topics such as abortion and eminent domain. These are important issues, no doubt, but we seem to have forgotten some of the other matters these new justices will be asked to decide. These judges will decide cases that interpret the Patriot Act. They will be asked to decide whether this nation can run intelligence operations like Able Danger, an ultra-secret Special Forces intelligence unit that was hunting for terror cells inside the United States. There will be crucial war-related decisions, and yet no one seems to care.

I want us to get un-apathetic. I want Americans to get engaged. I want us pissed beyond measure, maybe even a bit irrational. This war and its burdens are currently being borne by our soldiers and their families and them alone. The rest of us are not doing our part. If this keeps up, we will lose this war.

More people voted for the latest winner of *American Idol* than they did for president. Millions marched for new immigration policies. Where are the millions marching in the street over Iraq and Afghanistan? Does that mean we protest? Go ahead. I hope it means we are going to get involved in a positive manner. But I really don't care *how*—just get off your asses, give a damn, and get out there and do something. Don't sit. Don't allow the apathy to continue. Get involved! If you don't get involved, a national election will be held in which Vietnam and not terrorism will be the main topic. . . . Oh, wait, that already happened. If you don't get involved, 23,000 men and women killed or wounded won't upset you. . . . Uh-oh, too late on that one too.

You live in the United States of America; you can speak your mind. If our leaders haven't motivated us to stay committed to the fight against terrorists, we need to speak up and let them know that our safety is our number one priority. As individuals, we can't do things like increase the funding to improve our railroad security, but we can sure as hell speak out to make certain our leaders know this needs to be done immediately.

The Minutemen, a group of men and women who had enough of the lack of response from our government, made the news by patrolling our borders because the government wasn't doing it. They couldn't fix the problem by themselves, of course, but at least they got the National Guard patrolling the Arizona border in helicopters.[11] And at least they got Congress discussing the issue. The discussions weren't all that fruitful—senators and congressmen spent so much time bickering about the issues that they came up with a half-assed solution, as we'll see in Chapter 7—but it was a start. The border issue isn't going to fade away.

Plus we've got a problem with our troops: not enough of them. Our current troops are brave and tough as nails, but they're also exhausted. There aren't enough of them to meet the threats we face. People get all excited now when the military happens to hit its recruitment targets. The Army did just that in 2006. Too bad we've had to lower our standards to get there. According to the military's own data, 17 percent of the new recruits received educational, medical, moral, or criminal waivers. That means we're letting in a bunch of people who've had drug or alcohol problems, who've been arrested, or who couldn't even meet the basic aptitude standards.[12] Not too comforting.

So what does this have to do with us? Well, that's the issue—it shouldn't be *us*, the people here at home, and *them*, the small group of people we send overseas to protect us and our way of life. We know we need more troops, at least when we bother to think about the military. Yet no one wants to talk about a draft. No, it is not a dirty word; it is the word that means we all share in the responsibility to keep our citizens safe.

We have not given our soldiers the right gear with which to fight. They must buy their own and no one seems to care.

We spend our time watching coverage of one missing nineteen-year-old in Aruba because it distracts us from the things we don't want to face. There is a price for liberty. The preservation of our way of life requires that we care, that we pay attention, and that we, on occasion, make sacrifices in order to achieve the safety and security necessary for us to continue. We aren't doing it, but we must.

CHAPTER 5

THESE GUYS ARE SERIOUS

This is not the same kind of war our fathers fought. There are no bat-tlefields, no battle lines, and no rules governing the enemy's conduct. Terrorists strike anywhere, anytime, and in unconventional ways. While this sometimes leads us to think that their tactics are not sophisticated and that we can pummel them into the ground with sophisticated weaponry, we can't. Taking the fight to the enemy often means fighting them on their own turf, be it in high mountain plains or in house-to-house city fighting. It also means combating their tactics.

Even though we have made Iraq part of the War on Terror when it need not have been, there is some benefit to fighting there. Terrorists and insurgents use similar tactics, so our guys are getting invaluable combat experience that will aid us in this generational global War on Terror.

What kind of tactics and tools do the terrorists use? The insurgents in Iraq and terrorists around the world use suicide bombers, impro-vised explosive devices (IEDs), kidnappings, and snipers. And that's just the beginning. Really, there is no end to what these guys will use or do when trying to kill us. We need to recognize this and be willing to fight back on all fronts, with all of the tools at our disposal.

You probably recognize at least some of the tools mentioned above from the grisly TV coverage we see daily. Kidnappings, for example, have been widely covered by the broadcast and print media. We have all seen the videos of hostages reading letters of confession for the supposed crimes of the infidels, and then their masked captors cutting off their heads. It is a gruesome tactic designed to instill fear. It works.

After the Palestinian terrorist organization Black September killed eleven Israeli athletes during the 1972 Summer Olympics, Israel swept into action. The Israeli government put together a covert hit team to track down those responsible for the murders. The elite hit team traveled the world, and in the end killed more than a dozen members of Black September.

There were some mistakes, and at least one innocent was killed, but the Israeli government was right to do this. I wish our government were as aggressive. Unfortunately, we are afraid of making mistakes and getting bad publicity. Listen, there will always be mistakes; no one is perfect. Since when is a screw-up the signal to pack it in? If that were the case, Americans would never even have tried after Pearl Harbor, nor would the British have tried after Dunkirk. We would have given up after 9/11. We learn from our screw-ups, we admit to them, and then we cowboy the hell up. Otherwise, we might as well just stay in bed and get our asses kicked.

We need to follow the Israeli way of fighting kidnappers and hostage takers—we kill the perpetrators. Every time someone takes a hostage, we find out who did it, we hunt them down, and we kill them, even if it takes years. We train teams to do this job. We stay ready, and we always make those responsible for these acts pay with their lives. Going after those who have killed our citizens sends a clear message to the terrorists: *We may not get you all, we may fail to stop you totally, but we will not "go gentle into that good night"; we will kill you whenever and wherever we find you.* It shows the terrorists that they have attacked a country that cares enough to fight back.

This also sends a clear message to the nation that has been attacked by terrorists: *Your government is not impotent and cowardly. We did not start this, but we will damn sure finish it.*

Terrorists also need to know that the United States will *never* pay for the release of a hostage. More than 300 non-Iraqi people have been taken hostage since the coalition forces entered in 2003. Anyone care to guess what's happened to them? You might not know the answer because we haven't spent a lot of time publicizing this particular embarrassment. But the fact is, the French, the Germans, the British, the Italians, and even some U.S. companies have not only negotiated for the release of more than 70 percent of these hostages but paid for their release!

Hostage taking has become a cottage industry in Iraq. Why? Because when you pay people a lot of money for illegal activity, it tends to keep happening. Don't get me wrong. I'm not blaming the victim here; the people taking hostages are evil terrorists, plain and simple. But you can't do anything that provides further incentives to the terrorists. Once you start paying, you open yourself up to further kidnappings and murders. We are paying people to blow us up!

A U.S. government classified report made public in November 2006 demonstrates my point. It showed that the bad guys have brought in $36 million a year from ransoms paid for kidnap victims. Our "friends" Italy and France have contributed to this fund-raising effort. Well, isn't this nice. No longer do those killing American service members and Iraqi children have to depend on the largesse of Iran and Syria; these killers can now finance themselves. What this means, my friends, is that the bad guys can go on indefinitely; with this kind of money they can woo plenty of recruits. This is why allowing people to pay ransoms, and tolerating corruption, bribes, and crime, can sustain an insurgency.

We need to find and kill all hostage takers. We need to hunt them down no matter how long it takes. We can never let them escape. When we kill hostage takers, we should bring reporters on the takedown. Get those cameras rolling! We need to let everyone see what happens to those who take our citizens. We need to show the world that we mean what we say. Right now, that message is muffled if not mute.

SUICIDE BOMBINGS

When it comes to combating terrorist tactics, there are a few other things we could learn from the Israelis. They have been living with and fighting terrorism for years, so they know a thing or two. One thing they definitely know about is suicide bombers. Suicide bombers are indiscriminate, hateful murderers who strap explosives onto their bodies and walk into a crowd, a police station, or a pizza parlor, push a button, and blow themselves and anyone around them into small pieces. The Israelis also understand that suicide bombers are almost impossible to stop—note the word *almost.*

The Israelis have become experts at identifying bombers. Israel's intelligence services have studied every single suicide bomber's family history, what they looked like, how they smelled, how they dressed, what time of day the bombing occurred, what they weighed—*everything.* Now the Israelis train all their cops in what to look for: what the eyes of a suicide bomber look like, what the bombers wear—anything that will help them detect the next nutcase with a bomb strapped to him.

Hey, how about we learn from them? After all, suicide bombers are killing our people in Afghanistan and Iraq. And if that isn't a good enough reason to learn all we can about them, how about the fact that suicide bombers blew up trains and buses in London and Madrid? We should know that it is only a matter of time before it happens here. We must listen to those who know how to fight certain threats and have shown us they can be successful. I believe we should add the Israeli military to our forces and use their spies and police tactics. The Muslim world won't like that. But you know what? Tough shit! We're talking life and death here. Besides, don't kid yourself—the Muslim world is already gunning for Israel and for us. Look at what happened in July 2006, when the terrorist army of Hezbollah—which has been getting $100 million a year from Iran—began a war with Israel by launching rockets and kidnapping two Israeli soldiers. How much of a difference can it make to these bastards that we're getting advice from Israel when they already are actively working to make us dead?

We've got to figure out a way at least to cut down on suicide bombings because they are one of the terrorists' favorite tools. Suicide bombings are so prevalent for the simple reason that they're relatively easy and inexpensive to pull off. A bomber can conceal the explosives he's carrying by loading them in the pockets of a vest that he wears around his torso. The vests can be made cheaply—for only a few hundred dollars, or even less. The terrorist group Tamil Tigers in India perfected these vests, which have become ubiquitous because they are so effective and so deadly. Many terrorists now add ball bearings to the explosives in order to produce fragmentation and thus increase the range of the bombs.

THE WAR FOR TECHNOLOGY

But the insurgents in Iraq and other terrorists do not have to kill themselves in order to inflict damage on us. By using other kinds of IEDs, the insurgents do tremendous harm to our service members and security personnel, as well as to Iraqi civilians. IEDs are homemade or improvised devices designed to cause death or injury by using explosives alone or in combination with toxic chemicals, biological toxins, or radiological material. They have become the most effective killing machine within the terrorists' arsenal.

There exists a wide variety of IEDs, all of them lethal. They can use almost any type of material and initiator. IEDs can be configured as packages that are placed in roadways, hidden in potholes, thrown from overpasses, and so forth. These so-called roadside bombs can be detonated by the weight of passing vehicles, by command through time-delay devices, or by remote control. Using two-way radios, cell phones, garage door openers, and other remote devices has enabled the terrorists to become even more efficient killing machines, since they can watch from a distance and set off their bombs at the opportune moment. Standing in the distance also allows the killers not to compromise themselves.[1]

IEDs can be vehicle-borne as well—that is, trucks, cars, and even carts can be loaded with large amounts of explosives. These are even deadlier than roadside bombs.[2] To realize the extent of the death and destruction vehicle-borne IEDs can inflict, consider that they have been responsible for some of the biggest terrorist attacks in recent years: the 1993 World Trade Center bombing, the 1995 Oklahoma City bombing, the 1998 attacks on the U.S. embassies in Africa, and the 2000 USS *Cole* attack. According to explosives specialist Jeffrey A. Slotnick, IEDs were involved in more than 13,000 incidents between 1993 and 1997.[3]

By October 2006, more than 1,000 Americans in Iraq had been killed by IEDs. As many as 57 have been killed in a single month, and 30 to 40 are regularly murdered per month by IEDs.[4] As long as terrorists are willing to die for the "faith" or cause, the inexpensive, easily produced IED will continue to be one of their main weapons of choice.

Cell phone technology is becoming so advanced that terrorists can use it for much more than improving their IEDs. I recently met a limo driver who is able to track, from his cell phone, the time, altitude, destination, and arrival of any flight within the United States. He showed me how he does this; it was accurate to the minute. It listed things like "Flight X is at 10,000 feet descending over Providence, Rhode Island, hitting runway 101." Terrorists can easily purchase this tool; it is a product on the open market.

Global Positioning System (GPS) technology, which is basically a whiz-bang adaptation of the standard compass, has become another key tool for the terrorists. A GPS device not only can tell its user which way is north but also can determine the user's exact location on the planet within three meters. It operates by interacting with orbiting satellites to calculate location. By adding topographical and even neighborhood and street maps, the device can prepare a route to navigate past border patrols. Radical terrorist groups in Saudi Arabia have been offering classes to foreign fighters on how to navigate with GPS devices. These classes have even been posted on the Internet to instruct other jihadists and Islamo-fascists on how to use these devices to infiltrate Iraq and target specific sites and populations within the country.

Know where this stuff is made? Right here in the United States, in Kansas City, Missouri. This is another example of a tool developed for the military that has been co-opted for use by the public and has now fallen into the hands of the nut bags.

Another tool that spells disaster for the United States is laser technology. Green or red light shining in the eyes of airline pilots is not a joke; it is a serious and menacing act. Lasers are the guiding beams and the path to launch a missile. Despite all the attention paid to airport security since 9/11, we have done next to nothing to secure our airports against terrorist use of laser technology. At every airport in the United States, approach and takeoff paths and major runways remain essentially unprotected. It is only a matter of time before the next laser has a missile attached to it.

We already have the technology to combat this threat. All El Al (the Israeli airline) aircraft and the president's planes are already equipped with the necessary protection. It amounts to anti-laser and anti-missile pods that sit underneath airplanes and are connected to heat-sensing radar, automatically deploying when there is a threat and releasing debris to distract the missiles. We need to make this a priority, but this equipment is military-grade and very expensive. In fact, it will cost about $10 billion. But this equipment already exists! Unfortunately, we probably won't put the technology into all our civilian airplanes until one is taken out by a terrorist with a laser beam.

We are the most technologically advanced society on the planet. Are you telling me that we can't find a way to get the IED devices under control in Iraq, a way to circumvent GPS devices, laser beams, and so on? Instead of putting the best minds to work on these problems, what did we do instead? We formed a committee, put a high-powered general in charge, added a pile of spies and engineers to the mix, and voilà—they planned to . . . *discuss the issue.*

This brain trust has stopped nothing. They've only decided when they will meet again. Great, I'm impressed! There is no excuse for this—none, *nada*. For all the useless meetings, we got nothing. We must harness our technology to save soldiers' lives, stop foreign combatants from flooding into Iraq, and counter the threat of laser technology in terrorist hands. We must do it *now*! We can do almost anything when we put our minds to it—how about we decide to do this?

THE TERRORISTS' PATH TO "DEFINITIVE VICTORY"

Want to know how serious these guys are? Look at how they train their snipers in Iraq.

Snipers are lethal in Iraq because so much of the warfare is conducted in the alleys and backstreets of Iraqi cities. The terrorists who occupy the serpentine city blocks lie in wait for U.S. units on low rooftops and in doorways. That's why the Iraqi insurgents place so much emphasis on sniper training. They maintain Web sites that contain detailed instructions for their recruits about how to become snipers and how to inflict the maximum damage on the infidels. America's snipers are the best in the world, trained to stalk their prey, conceal their own movements, spot telltale signs of an enemy shooter, and take down a target with a single shot.[5] The Defense Department has distributed a document to U.S. commanders in Iraq revealing that the insurgency has begun training snipers to rival those of the American military.

Tactically, the insurgents' sniper training is quite similar to our own, but the philosophy behind the training reveals how different their strategy is from ours. It's chilling to read how the terrorists target U.S. military targets.

Take one of the first commandments to the terrorist sniper: "Target the head of the snake and then handicap the command of the enemy." Why? Because, the manual instructs, replacing officers and commanders takes lots of time and money for the Americans, since it costs "more than $500,000" and requires four years to put a person through "the famous West Point college."

The manual also gives a serious admonition to snipers: U.S. Special

Forces "are very stupid because they have a 'Rambo complex,' thinking that they are the best in the world; don't be arrogant like them." Oh, and it says the terrorists should kill those arrogant Rambo bastards too.

Make no mistake, these terrorists are cold-eyed killers. Yeah, a bunch of them will blow themselves up in suicide bombings, but they also are very strategic in devising lethal ways to eliminate the hated Americans. It's especially revealing to look at a "training exercise" in the manual that shows a bunch of pictures of American soldiers and politicians and asks, "Who would you shoot? . . . If you had only one shot, who should you kill?" The manual then gives the answers, including such gems as this: "If you see a line of Soldiers, kill the one who you think is the officer. Then, shoot the communications officer, then the MG [machine gunner]—then the doctor—if he's there, you'll know by the red cross on his arm—(you don't need to respect the Geneva Treaty as long as the enemy does not respect it) and shoot at the Soldiers."

Do you get it? The terrorists are totally focused on one thing—*killing us.*

Oh, but maybe that sniper manual doesn't make it clear enough. Well, how about al-Qaeda's "seven-phase plan for world conquest"? Does that give you a good indication of what's driving the terrorists? Jordanian journalist Fouad Hussein revealed the plan after interviewing top al-Qaeda lieutenants for his 2005 book *Al-Zarqawi: Al-Qaeda's Second Generation*. The terrorist leader Abu Musab al-Zarqawi is now dead, of course, but make no mistake, the grand plan remains in place. Here's how these seven phases roll out:

Phase 1, "The awakening": The terrorists use attacks like 9/11 to provoke the United States into declaring war on the Islamic world, which will mobilize Islamic radicals, getting them to rally around al-Qaeda. Al-Qaeda considers this phase complete.

Phase 2, "Opening eyes": During this period, which Hussein said would last until the end of 2006, the terrorists continue to form their secret battalions and show Muslims how to wage war on the "infidels" and the "Western conspiracy."

Phase 3, "Arising and standing up": This phase, which should last until 2010, will bring increasingly frequent attacks against secular Turkey and archenemy Israel. The aroused Muslims will go to war against the infidels, and the devastation that Israel will face will force world leaders to negotiate with al-Qaeda.

Phase 4, "The downfall": This period will last until 2013 and will see the fall of hated Arab regimes, including Saudi Arabia and Jordan. Oil suppliers will be attacked and the U.S. economy will be targeted with cyberterrorism. Al-Qaeda will control the Persian Gulf, the oil, and most of the Middle East, giving them enough power and resources to attack the U.S. economy and military forces.

Phase 5, "The caliphate": Sometime between 2013 and 2016, al-Qaeda will establish the caliphate—that is, one government for all Muslim nations. All Western influences will be eliminated from the Muslim world. The caliphate will organize an army for the next phase.

Phase 6, "Total world conquest": Beginning in 2016, the Islamic army will begin the "fight between the believers and the nonbelievers" that Osama bin Laden has predicted. By 2022, the rest of the world will be conquered by the mighty and unstoppable armies of Islam.

Phase 7, "Definitive victory": By 2025, the army of "one and a half billion Muslims" will have proven their superiority. All the world's inhabitants will be forced to convert to Islam or be ruled by the caliphate as second-class citizens.[6]

I repeat: how safe do you feel now?

Actually, there are bigger questions: If we know all this about the terrorists, their capabilities, and their intentions, why don't we respond appropriately? Why have we allowed the war to become politicized, when real leaders would be focused on the task at hand—killing the bad guys?

Unfortunately, our leadership in this war has not stepped up to the challenge. In Iraq, a Navy SEAL element, a Special Forces company, or a Delta Force squadron could open up the airport road in less than a month; they could clear an entire town the size of Basra and maintain the peace with their Iraqi counterparts there in six months; they could stop infiltrators along a section of border immediately. They could do magic if only they were allowed to do their jobs. So how in hell was an entire Navy SEAL element allowed to sit on their powerful, perfectly trained asses for an entire year? They did next to nothing—even though they begged for a mission and are the best in the world at what they do. They sat on their asses because their leaders and their leaders' leaders are risk-averse, PowerPoint-briefing, politically correct, do-nothing assholes. The SEAL element actually gained weight on a deployment when they usually lose ten pounds per man.

This is wrong; this is how we lose. This is how an insurgency grows and a civil war materializes.

LOSING THE PR WAR

We also lose because we don't fight the public relations war properly. Terrorists run their own PR campaigns. They use fear and religious rhetoric to recruit or frighten citizens into supporting their causes. They use TV, radio, and the Internet to get their message out to the minions. They put up posters warning their countrymen not to vote because polling places are considered legitimate targets for attacks.

Al-Qaeda's Jihad Committee in Iraq—the group that was led by Abu Musab al-Zarqawi until our guys killed him—has been leading the propaganda war. Not only are the terrorists murdering our soldiers, but they're trying to win the hearts and minds of the people of Iraq and the rest of the Middle East. In an attempt to rally Sunni Arabs to their cause and to derail the American campaign for democracy, al-Qaeda has delivered some startling messages. Take a look at some of the things they've printed on their posters:

Those who fail to implement the laws of Allah are infidels.
Do not become easy prey for the crusaders.

Whoever fails to rule by what Allah has ordered,
then they are infidels.
Allah
Elections
Democracy
Constitution[7]

As a nation, if we know nothing else, we know how to wage political wars. We do it all the time here in the United States. We need to export this talent to the places where we are fighting terrorists. We should be designing counter-campaigns to make fun of and diminish the terrorist leaders. We need to put up posters of our own and spread rumors, true or untrue; this is one of those moments when all is fair in love and war (or at least the war part). If presidential candidates here in the United States can slam each other nonstop and sling all kinds of mud, we should be able to trash nut jobs who have made it their mission in life to murder Americans and other "infidels."

Think these messages won't work? Well, maybe not alone, but when we pump money and equipment and help into countries in combination with a good PR campaign, it certainly does help. Don't forget what happened in Indonesia after we swept in with aid and relief following the devastating tsunami: those with a favorable view of the United States nearly tripled, Indonesia became the first Muslim country to have more of its population supporting the War on Terror than opposing it, and support for bin Laden dropped sharply.[8]

We also need to take a good hard look at our friends and enemies.

For example, on the enemy front, there are the Iranians. They are supplying terrorists in Iraq with explosively formed projectiles (EFPs). These amazingly simple and devastatingly powerful weapons blow holes in heavily armored vehicles using what is basically a metal plate that can be shot out of a cannon. EFPs are killing our guys, and Iran is behind it.[9]

The first thing we need to do is modify our vehicles to resist the effects of EFPs—something we could do if the private sector threw money at the problem. But we could also deal with the source of the problem, Iran. We have tools in our political arsenal that could deal with Iran, at least at this level of weaponry, without us having to face fighting a war on another front. For starters, how about we get some other countries to apply pressure on the Iranians? Yeah, I know, easier said than done. But look at the Russians and Chinese: we have things they need, whether it's money or access or whatever. Let's get them to the table for a change. It ain't pretty, but sometimes you've got to make deals behind the scenes to get things done. And stopping support for terrorism must get done.

It is time to make the countries that support the terrorists pay a price that would make them think long and hard about helping those who wish to destroy the West.

GET IT DONE AND GET IT WON

The terrorists are serious. Are we?

We don't have any choice but to get just as serious as they are. We need to look at how we, as a nation, wage war. We don't employ enough snipers. We don't cross enough borders when we know supply routes and escape routes lie within other sovereign nations. We don't use false information. We don't pay for the equipment that would protect our soldiers. We don't use the power of a mobilized American people behind this war. We don't use religion as a weapon—by getting religious leaders to speak on our behalf, spying inside mosques and cathedrals, following people from religious services and tagging their cars, putting cameras inside houses of worship, and in general taking religion off the do-not-touch list and letting everyone know it. We don't use all our weapons, even all our government, to focus on one thing—winning this war. We don't act like this fight is what it really is: total war. This is all wrong.

Hell, as of today we have not officially declared war. We talk about war. We make speeches using the word *war*. But Congress hasn't even bothered to declare war. That is wrong.

To declare war in this country requires our leaders to work along two tracks, one political, the other social. The political is obvious: the president makes his case to Congress, Congress votes, and abracadabra—we are at war. The social is more difficult. The same president must convince the public that the war is necessary and justified because of the tools the terrorists use and their plans for the future demise of our nation. But when the president does this successfully, he gets more political power and the moral authority to do whatever it takes to win the war.

You can't—or at least shouldn't be allowed to—use the W word when war hasn't been declared. The political types do it anyway. But the bad guys know our laws and our ways; they know we haven't declared war. Without the declaration of war, terrorists can hide in places like Pakistan or Iran and we do nothing about it. If we were at war, they couldn't hide. Those who have been in a declared war—the last one was World War II—know the difference. That generation, although supportive, shakes its collective head at us.

Declare war, dammit! Be done with it and get it won!

CHAPTER 6

ARE WE PREPARED?

The iron fist of Islamic radicals hit this country on 9/11. Now more than ever, our government must be responsive and capable of protecting its citizens. We know it's only a matter of time before the bad guys hit us again. Our country is too damned big for us to be 100 percent effective at stopping every attack, no matter how good we get at intelligence and at tracking down terrorists. So we need to know our government is able to help us if and when a disaster strikes.

When we talk about the government, we usually think of the guys in Washington. That makes sense, because the federal government, which controls that monstrosity we call the Department of Homeland Security, does play a major role in ensuring our safety and providing relief when disaster arrives. But the feds aren't the only ones responsible. The truth is that local authorities are the first to respond when disaster strikes. They are there when things go wrong. They are the closest. They get the call first.

That's why "Be prepared" should be the motto not just for the Boy Scouts but also for our entire country.

Each city and state in this great nation has to have some plan, some idea, some thought about how they will react to a catastrophic event. They need to have a plan because the scary truth about acts of terrorism—and acts of God too—is that you never know where or when they will happen. Right now, we assume that terrorists want to attack the United States in the biggest and boldest way possible. That's true! But if those kinds of attacks become too difficult to pull off, they could easily turn to making smaller attacks possible anywhere.

What if: *In Lawton, Oklahoma, at the New Gate shopping mall, a suicide bomber blows himself up, killing forty-seven innocent bystanders.*

How about: *In Newton, Massachusetts, an upscale mall is attacked with anthrax. Those infected wind up at the six area hospitals, which results in the infection of thousands.*

Maybe it will be: *In Fairmont, California, a switch is blown, setting off a chain of events and causing a blackout throughout the West. The subsequent murders, robberies, and car accidents create chaos.*

Don't think places like that are vulnerable? How about a small town in Maine? Not a very big terrorist target, right? Well, what if this same small town has a restaurant frequented by the Bush family, who happens to live a few miles down the coast? Each town or city knows best what its specific vulnerabilities are. The key questions are: How are we addressing those vulnerabilities? Are we prepared to cope if something catastrophic does happen?

We need to be prepared because if we are not, we could die, our children could die, our mothers, our fathers, and everyone else we know could die. This means that even those of you residing in Bat Cave, North Carolina, you've got to have a plan! Bangor, Maine, you've got to have a plan! And Los Angeles, *for sure,* you've got to have a plan!

But do we have a plan? Are we prepared to deal with catastrophe? Before you answer too quickly, let me throw one word at you: *Katrina.*

Hurricane Katrina was a disaster brought to us by Mother Nature, not by terrorists. But our government's response to that 2005 storm indicates how ill-prepared our government is to deal with catastrophe. Remember, we saw this one coming for days. Our satellites and planes tracked the killer since its birth. We saw it; we tested it; we measured it;

we smelled it. Our government told us, *No problem. We've got this one covered. We're prepared. We're doing our jobs. Trust us!*

Yeah, right. Guess what happened next.

THE FAILED TEST

Hurricane Katrina was one humongous storm, a huge mutha that brought tons of rain, waves in biblical proportion, and winds that toppled buildings. It was a catastrophe on steroids. But it was a catastrophe we saw coming, and therefore we should have been prepared.

The National Hurricane Center, a part of the National Weather Service, issued its first advisory about Katrina (then a tropical depression) on Tuesday, August 23, 2005, six days before the storm made landfall along the Gulf Coast. That was the first of roughly thirty different advisories the center would issue over the next several days. By Friday morning, August 26, the center was warning that Katrina could become a "major hurricane." That same morning, the center held a conference call with the Federal Emergency Management Agency (FEMA) headquarters. On Saturday the Hurricane Center held video-conferences not only with FEMA headquarters but also with state officials in Louisiana, Mississippi, Alabama, Georgia, and Florida. The center made it clear that Katrina could make landfall as a Category 4 or even Category 5 hurricane—the latter the most severe level of storm. Also on Saturday, two days prior to landfall, the director of the National Hurricane Center, Max Mayfield, personally called the governors of Mississippi and Louisiana as well as the mayor of New Orleans to warn them that Katrina was on a direct path toward them.[1]

On Sunday, August 28, the day before Katrina made landfall, Mayfield gave a videoconference briefing to federal officials in Washington and Crawford, Texas. He predicted that winds would smash windows in high-rise buildings and floodwaters would wipe out large sections of the Gulf Coast. He even warned that some of New Orleans' levees might not hold. National Weather Service meteorologist Paul Trotter reiterated the warnings the same day and predicted that "most of the area will be uninhabitable for weeks . . . perhaps longer."[2] Trotter even issued a public statement calling Katrina "a most powerful hurricane with unprecedented strength . . . rivaling the intensity of Hurricane Camille of 1969." Camille killed 256 people.[3]

So the federal, state, and local governments all knew what was coming. That included everyone from local emergency managers to FEMA to the president himself. State and local officials, having been briefed two days before Katrina came ashore, could have ordered an evacuation and prepared a suitable response if the worst-case scenario came to fruition. But they didn't. Evacuation could have begun at least thirty-six hours before the full fury of Katrina hit the Gulf coastline. But it didn't.

There was no communication or coordination among the three levels of government and their agencies. Food and shelters were not secured. This lack of preparation and coordination of relief efforts was the result of incompetence, plain and simple.

When the rain stopped and the clouds cleared, what did we see? (And by the way, we did see it all, because the national media and their cameras were there en masse.) We saw bodies floating in what used to be the low-lying streets of New Orleans, a city three-quarters under water. We saw large-scale looting and other rampant crime. And we saw more than 100,000 people—among them the city's poor, disabled, and infirm residents—left behind to face the hurricane and its aftermath without aid.

Evacuation plans had failed to take into account the one-third of New Orleans' population without transportation. No car equaled no hope. This should not have been a surprise, because a 2002 series in a New Orleans newspaper, the *Times-Picayune,* accurately predicted that if a major storm hit the city, getting out of town could be close to impossible for thousands of residents.[4]

The public buses that would transport people out of the city in the event of a disaster took people to the Louisiana Superdome instead. This sports arena was to be a staging point from which to transport people out of the state. But nearly a week after the hurricane hit the ground, thousands of people were still waiting for buses to take them out of the city. By then the Superdome had become uninhabitable because the air-conditioning was cut off, running water had stopped, and toilets were backed up. The stench of rotting bodies filled a shopping arcade leading from the Superdome out to an adjacent hotel. Survivors told of dumping corpses into the floodwaters around the arena, just to get them away from the living. Starving babies cried inconsolably as their mothers sat helpless because they were unable to feed them with the military rations they didn't even get until late in the week. The entire infrastructure had failed; there was no electricity, water, or food.

Care to guess whom the stranded, taxpaying, child-rearing, hardworking, mostly poor people were begging for help? Reporters and news personalities! Yes, news organizations had managed to do what the city, state, and all-powerful federal government could not do— *show the hell up.* For example, Fox News had Bill O'Reilly, Shepard Smith, and Geraldo Rivera pleading on television on behalf of the thousands who either refused to go, couldn't go, or were left behind. The media had to show our leaders the extent of the damage and prod them on international television before they got their act together and sent in the military to aid the victims.

There were amazingly heroic efforts by individuals, organizations, and certain branches of our government. But these efforts came in spite of, not because of, the Department of Homeland Security and its charge, FEMA. Church groups, the Red Cross, the U.S. Coast Guard, even Hollywood celebrities contributed. But the buses, food, and National Guard that were part of the overall FEMA plan were waiting outside the city. *Waiting!* Funny, the military blockade was lifted and FEMA entered the city right behind our commander in chief. Probably just a coincidence, not the photo opportunity some people have suggested.

What happened? The mayor of New Orleans didn't do his job, but he didn't have a problem pointing fingers at everyone else. The Police

Department and emergency response units all over the hurricane area were overwhelmed. This happened despite that very well-run and very expensive practice drill conducted the year before—Hurricane Pam. Didn't anyone read the report? Didn't anyone watch the training film that we paid for? It would appear that the only decision the governor of Louisiana could make was the one to cry on worldwide television. The president, who has since admitted to some government "missteps," was on a vacation in Texas. The FEMA director and Homeland Security chief should have been with him in Crawford considering the level of incompetence they demonstrated.

No one accepted responsibility, but we all know things got out of control because our leaders at all levels of government failed to do their jobs. They should all be fired! But hell, the mayor of New Orleans was actually *reelected*.

Our government failed the poor bastards on the Gulf Coast. It failed them at the local level, it failed them at the state level, and for five days it failed them at the federal level. And the entire world watched all this. They saw a country that looked inept and vulnerable.

The War on Terror is all about preparing for, and responding to, any attacks on American soil. The federal agencies who were in charge during Katrina—Homeland Security and FEMA—are the same agencies who will be responsible if we are attacked again. How we handled this natural disaster—one for which we had ample warning—does not bode well for us. Not at all.

WE NEED A PLAN

So what do we do? If we failed the Katrina test—and we failed it badly—how in the world can we be ready if, or when, the terrorists hit us again?

Preparedness has to work across all levels of government—local, state, and federal—and across all agencies. Everyone plays a part, including each citizen. People should know what is expected of them during an emergency. Right this second, as you are reading this, ask yourself these questions:

- If you were ordered to evacuate your home, where are you supposed to go?
- If you don't know, why don't you know?
- Do the leaders of your town know?
- Is there a plan in place?

Maybe you want to put down this book and pick up the phone to find out.

Preparedness really begins at the local level, with you and me and our fellow townspeople. Once a town or city has figured out how vulnerable it is, the residents must decide what security plan is possible. They need to decide how much money they have to spend on the plan, and then they need to combine that with money they receive from the state and federal governments. All these funds need to be used to ensure the most effective security.

There is always one essential ingredient within any successful plan: first responders must have the ability to communicate with each other within and outside the immediate disaster area. If you can't talk to each other, you can't help each other and you damned sure can't figure out what to do. We found this out during Hurricane Katrina. William Lokey, FEMA's chief of response operations, told senators during their investigation of Katrina that other federal departments' offers to help rescue storm victims went unheard or ignored. Lokey testified that "communications and coordination was lacking, preplanning was lacking."[5]

That problem, lack of communication, still exists. FEMA and other federal agencies still haven't made changes in the use of phone and radio channels to facilitate effective communication in a crisis. Right now, the federal government is the single controlling source of who gets what phone and radio frequencies. Our police, fire, and National Guard can't talk to each other. Hell, they can't talk to themselves on any single emergency frequency. This is after five years of spouting about how "we are safer."

Care to guess who has come up with a fix? It's none other than a Democrat, a senator from Delaware named Joe Biden. The fix is rather complicated, but simply put, it would require an expansion of the channels designated for public safety. By converting the analog signals to digital, we'd make many more channels available and would secure certain channels for the exclusive use of the responders. In other words, they would be able to talk to one another and messages would get through. Also, the signal quality would be significantly improved. Biden proposed this as early as 1997 as part of the Balanced Budget Act of 1997. The 9/11 Commission also urged Congress to take steps to ensure greater communication capacity. So let's get it done. For crying out loud, what are we paying Homeland Security for? I don't care *who* fixes this stuff or how much it costs as long as it gets fixed, and gets fixed now.

We've got several possible solutions to the communications problem, but satellite radios are the best. These gadgets bounce their signals from communication satellites to receivers or other radios. They don't depend on wires, telephone poles, or electricity. You simply point the radio in the direction of the satellite and bingo, you have communication.

When you don't use this technology, you get another New Orleans. Does your town or city have satellite radios? Don't know? How confident are you feeling now?

We need to make sure our cities have this equipment. It's expensive but necessary. This type of communication equipment for thirty large cities would cost approximately $1 billion. That's a lot of money! But it's only one-eighth of the $8 billion we spend each year on Star Wars. The expenditure makes sense if our government is intent on prioritizing programs that can make us safer in the face of terrorism.

Beyond adequate emergency communications systems, we need to ensure that our institutions can be depended upon in a security crisis. Hospitals are critical when talking about a security plan. Currently, hospitals are great for everyday things: operations, giving out medicine, charging huge amounts of money. Yet few, if any, are ready to handle fifty new sick people an hour for twenty-four hours, or worse, the mass casualties and wounded that might be the result of an attack. To do that, and do it well, takes training.

The first task of the medical disaster response team is to identify the true nature of the incident. Damaged infrastructure and inadequate communication technology will necessarily affect the response. Right now, in most cases, we depend on often-unreliable telephonic and two-way radio communication among ambulances, hospitals, and the incident command central. In a biological attack, we need to recognize the agent, control the infection, and have adequate personnel, facilities, supplies, and antidotes. And this just scratches the surface of the immense problems that our medical services would face in any major disaster.

So what can we do? The experts—including the Centers for Disease Control, state and local health departments, the American Medical Association, the Federation of Medicine, and major hospitals—must run a complete assessment of the problems and the solutions, and train medical response teams in all area hospitals.

What happens if we have large-scale human-to-human transmission of bird flu? How long would it take for us to recognize it? How would we handle quarantines? A severe influenza outbreak would be a catastrophe; what word is there to describe a bird flu epidemic? It would take us days just to recognize it and more days for the federal government to react. Probably the first thing the federal government would do would be to impose quarantine. That means casualties would rise and there would be no school, no work, no shopping malls, and no moving from your town. Envision tanks on the freeway. Your local National Guard will become your jailer. We don't want this to happen, anytime or anywhere in this country. How do we prevent this scenario? Prepare and practice, practice, practice emergency response. The Boy Scouts' motto comes to mind again.

Schools also need to practice evacuation. They need to practice crowd control. How many schools in your area have taught the kids that in an emergency, when the school is in lockdown, approaching the windows is a bad thing? In Beslan, Russia, 186 kids died when terrorists attacked a school. The disaster was due to incompetence and poor planning. The first responders of the Russian federal government never showed up; there were only the well-intentioned but incompetent local rescuers. As a result, innocent kids were killed. This Russian tragedy should have been a huge wake-up call for us, but here we say we are better than those damn Russians. It could never happen here!

Really? Is it possible that we have forgotten Columbine or the assault on the Amish school? It could happen here; it *has* happened here.

THE MODEL

One city has shown us the way we can solve problems and make our homes safer. It is the city that was hit the hardest, has lost more citizens, has sustained more damage, and has been targeted with the most attention since 9/11. Of course I am talking about the great city of New York.

New York's police department has done more than any other in the country to be prepared for the next attack. Through their hard work and innovations, the police have been able to bring relative calm to their traumatized population. The NYPD blue uniform is what the millions of New York residents trust way before any bureaucrat from the federal government.

Dynamic leadership on the part of elected officials who have shown real care and concern accomplished this. Even if New York City hadn't been attacked on 9/11, it would have eventually had to become the armed camp it is today, because it is the most recognized city in the world. It is the symbol of all that is good and bad in the United States. No other city in this country has spent the money, hired the most-qualified people, or done the planning, coordination, and practice necessary to prepare for what *could happen* that New York has. All cities and towns should learn from New York's hard work.[6]

The city has done a remarkable job preparing for the inevitable. When terrorists struck London in the summer of 2005, New York leaped into action. Municipal law enforcement personnel leaves were cancelled, the night shift didn't go home, and a cop was put on every train. Behind the scenes there were many others who were working just as hard to sift through incoming intelligence and working sources—listening to the street.

One of the big reasons New York has done well is that the city hasn't been afraid to look for ideas and people outside the traditional police world. New York's top cop, Ray Kelly, made a former CIA guy one of the deputy chiefs of police and made a former Marine another. Kelly then went to the Israelis and said, "We need your help." The Israelis gave him access to real-time intelligence, armed tactical training for the city's SWAT team, and training in terrorist profiling for New York City detectives. In addition, Kelly established liaison teams made up of New York City police officers who had lived in Israel, London, Paris, Moscow, and other hot spots. The objective was to learn from those countries' intelligence agencies and police departments. These teams feed information directly to the New York Police Department when there is even a hint of a terrorist strike against their fair city. Commissioner Kelly also had Arabic-speaking and other language-skilled officers assigned to computer teams to check the Web for any sign of "chatter" indicating an attack.

The bottom line is that New York City has become the model for how to combat terrorism.

FIXING OUR MISTAKES

Preparedness begins on the local level, but it can't end there. The state and federal governments play an essential role in protecting us. The state's role is mainly supportive. It can deploy the National Guard to areas to help in times of crisis. It supplies money and equipment and command centers. It acts as a liaison to the federal government. The state's most important work should happen *before* disaster strikes.

The state allocates the money so that localities can get the equipment, training, and expertise they need to be prepared. How much money is your town being given to get prepared? Don't know? Maybe you should find out.

Because of Hurricane Katrina, many people have begun to ask what the federal government's role is when we are hit by a terrorist attack or natural disaster. What its role should *not* be is to screw things up. In 2006, internal government memos surfaced showing that the feds were providing only 25 percent of the requested supplies to the field during Hurricane Katrina. By any standard, 25 percent gets a grade of F. The head of FEMA had to be informed on TV by a reporter that there were people waiting to be helped at the Superdome in New Orleans. So, after $170 billion, when Americans needed their government's help, those in charge were getting their information from Fox News and other networks? What a great plan.

If done correctly, pre-positioning of disaster relief supplies can lessen the impact of a disaster and ward off much of the resulting suffering. Pre-positioning these supplies in places you can't get to doesn't help at all. But that's what our government did for Katrina: it put 40,000 housing trailers that were needed in Louisiana . . . *in Arkansas*. They are still there today. This is unforgivable. The federal government's emergency response should never take longer than twenty-four hours. In New Orleans it took five days, and even then, the response was a poor effort.

The Department of Homeland Security is the biggest mistake our government made after 9/11. We knee-jerked an agency together and got exactly what comes of such boneheaded decisions—disaster. We took efficient agencies like the Coast Guard, the Secret Service, and FEMA and put them under one roof with a guy in charge who had no earthly idea what he was doing. When Hurricane Katrina struck, the Coast Guard went in and did what it does—it saved people. While everyone else was in a meeting and sending memos, the Coast Guard was actually doing something. FEMA, which used to be an incredibly capable organization, was lost in the red tape of Homeland Security. When it came time to replace the idiot in charge of FEMA—whose qualifications included being a lawyer and an Arabian horse competition judge—they picked the guy responsible for telling Americans that in the event of a chemical attack, the best way to protect themselves was with duct tape and plastic sheeting, R. David Paulison.

How about the Department of Homeland Security? We need to blow it up. Get rid of it. Scrap it. Make FEMA the arm of the federal government that responds to terrorist attacks and natural disasters and return it to its former state of competency. In April 2006, the Senate Homeland Security and Government Affairs Committee issued a report, "Hurricane Katrina: A Nation Still Unprepared," recommending that FEMA be dismantled.[7] FEMA was a responsible and capable agency when it was not an arm of Homeland Security, the real culprit in Katrina.

I have a saying, "Hope is not a method." But that is precisely what we are witnessing now. The feds hope that there won't be another Katrina anytime soon. Why? Because they haven't finished cleaning up from the last one. Truth is, no one should have gone back into the devastated areas until they were safe, but our government didn't have the balls to make that decision. So what are they doing? Hoping. Give me a break! FEMA used to know how to do this. They need to remember and get back to doing it.

There is a lot of discussion now about giving the military a larger role in disaster response. The president has actually said that he is considering putting the military in charge of this stuff. It shouldn't happen. When on U.S. soil, the only thing the military should do is support other agencies. This was how it worked before Homeland Security made a mess of things. The military, with all its capabilities, should never be in the lead in this country nor anywhere else. It should always be kept under civilian control—never a chance of a coup that way. This makes perfect sense and it works.

The government has crucial responsibilities for ensuring the safety of our country. How much of our security plan is being done right? Not nearly enough. We need to fix it before we face attacks that are bigger and more devastating than 9/11. We flunked the Katrina test, the bin Laden test, and many others. The world and the terrorist bottom-feeders were watching our miserable performance. Were you watching?

CHAPTER 7

WHAT YOU DON'T KNOW ABOUT OUR BORDERS

"We fight them over there so we don't have to fight them here."

Not sure who said this first, but it is a line we often hear when the talking heads and politicians take center stage to defend and explain our decision to go into Iraq. While it makes for a nice sound bite, it isn't true. The truth is we need to be fighting terrorists everywhere, all the time, if we are going to be successful in this War on Terror. And we sure as hell need to be waging war against them here at home because, as we have seen, the terrorists mean business and they show no sign of packing it in.

Let me put this simply: if the terrorists can't get their people or their weapons into our country, the chance that they will successfully launch attacks against us diminishes tenfold. Now, it's true that we will never be able to prevent every attack; to do so we would have to be right 100 percent of the time, which is impossible. The terrorists only have to get lucky once. But that doesn't mean we stop trying! Throwing up our hands—or tying them behind our back with bureaucratic red tape—is not a viable option.

If we are serious about protecting our country, and ourselves, we need to know who and what is entering, wandering around, and exiting our country. Right now, more than five years after 9/11, we have almost no clue about any of this.

At last count, there were between 11 million and 20 million illegal immigrants in this country. The truth is that those numbers are guesses; we don't really know how many are here. Every year between 1 million and 3 million illegal aliens run, jump, fly, swim, and drive across our borders. These people come from everywhere and we know nothing about them. Oh, sure, we work the piss out of some of these people— they wash our cars, cut our grass, and watch our kids. But we don't really know where they come from, where they go once they enter the country, or what they intend to do while they are here.

Here are the stark realities of the situation:

- The number of illegal immigrants in this country has surpassed the number of legal immigrants.
- Since 9/11 the number of illegal immigrants sneaking across our borders has increased.
- Since 9/11 the number of illegal immigrants from countries of "special interest," otherwise known as countries that sponsor terrorism, has increased. According to government formulas, 190,000 illegal immigrants from these countries melted into the U.S. population in 2004 alone.[1]

If safety is the issue, and safety *should* be the issue, then the number of illegal immigrants should be decreasing, not increasing. At the very least, the number of illegals from state sponsors of terror should be coming way down. One hundred and ninety thousand is not acceptable! These are not the signs of a government that is taking our safety seriously.

In October 2006, two weeks before the congressional elections, the president signed the Secure Fence Act. It should have been called the Useless Fence Act, or Part of a Fence Act, or how about the Pretend There Is a Fence to Get Your Vote Act? When it comes to the business of protecting this country, partial solutions never work. This supposed fence we will probably never build is proposed to be 700 miles long, which seems like a lot until you realize that the border is more than twice that size. Oh, and then there is the fact that there is only funding for 300 miles of the 700-mile imaginary fence. Half a fence, unfunded border patrol jobs—and all of this five years after 9/11.

The politicians in Washington can't even agree that we need to know who is here and why. Everyone agrees what we have to do—get tougher. Washington hasn't done it. They all suck.

Sure, most illegal immigrants probably come here looking for jobs and a better life, or at least we *hope* they do. But remember, hope is not a method, and it is certainly not in our arsenal of security measures. Our leaky borders have enabled the bad guys to come here, live among us, and plan to carry out attacks against us. The bottom line is that we need to stop the flow of bad guys coming across our borders. In order to do this, we have to get control of everyone who comes here, whether they are well intentioned or not.

On November 25, 2002, the president signed the Homeland Security Act into law. This act did away with the Immigration and Naturalization Service (INS), which had handled the border situation. That enforcement responsibility was placed under the Directorate of Border Transportation Security, or Customs and Border Protection (CBP).

After reading that, can you tell me who is in charge of stopping people from crossing the border illegally, who inspects people and things coming across the border, who is charged with immigration and customs enforcement, or who investigates, detains, and/or removes illegal aliens? No? I'm not surprised. What do we actually know? We know that these tasks now fall *somewhere* under the Department of Homeland Security. These are the same people who are in charge of the airports. By the way, twenty-two airports were tested for security and failed. These are the same people who have done nothing to secure our trains and our bridges. These are the same people who have no idea how they will react to a chemical or biological disaster, whether man-made or natural. These are the same people who failed miserably during Hurricane Katrina. These are the same people who cannot combine all the terrorist watch lists into one list. These are the same people who have failed across the board at everything they have been tasked to do.

Really, how safe are you feeling now?

WE'VE GOT TWO BORDERS, REMEMBER?

We need to secure our borders—*both* of them. When we talk about people illegally crossing the borders into the United States, we are most often referring to Mexico. What about our other border? On June 4, 2006, Canadian authorities arrested seventeen young Muslim men who were plotting attacks against Canadian interests. The plot included plans to behead the Canadian prime minister. These guys were arrested because they procured three tons of ammonium nitrate, one of the raw materials used to manufacture explosives. Three tons is two more than Timothy McVeigh used to blow up the Oklahoma City Federal Building. Oh, and we already know about the presence of fifty different terrorist organizations in Canada. Given all that, we might want to start thinking a little more broadly when we talk about border security.

Or try this on for size: the Canadian border is at least twice as long as the Mexican border.[2] You can drive a boat the size of the *Queen Mary* down the coast of Maine from Canada and no one will stop you. You can drive a fleet of dump trucks through the border checkpoint and get waved through—on both sides—without ever being stopped.

Remember Ahmed Ressam, the Millennium Bomber? He was the Algerian terrorist arrested in December 1999 by U.S. customs agents in Port Angeles, Washington. This guy had more than 100 pounds of explosives hidden in the trunk of the rental car he had driven onto a ferry in Victoria, British Columbia, Canada. How did he get on the ferry in the first place? He showed U.S. immigration agents a fake Canadian passport, which passed a computer check. They even looked in the trunk of his car! But he got the all-clear. It was only when he got to the U.S. side that he aroused serious suspicion with hesitant answers to agents' questions. When they began searching his car, he tried to bolt. Our people caught him.[3]

But before you start patting people on the back, you might want to know that the Canadians had practically rolled out the red carpet for this terrorist. He had come to Canada in 1994, requesting political asylum. Even though he showed a pretty obviously false French passport, Canadian authorities accepted his plea and released him, pending a hearing on his refugee status. Apparently they never bothered to check out his story with Algeria, France, or Interpol. Nice work, boys! Had they done some investigating, they might have learned that he had joined a militant Islamic rebel organization in Algeria years earlier.

Once the Millennium Bomber got to Canada, he lived in an apartment building the police later identified as the Montreal headquarters of the Armed Islamic Group (GIA), a terrorist cell connected to Osama bin Laden's network. Over the course of four years, he was arrested for theft four times but never served a day in jail. Then he missed his hearing regarding his request for asylum. The Canadians issued a warrant for his arrest, but immigration authorities never tracked him down. He should have been deported, but instead he stayed and began providing Canadian passports to terrorists all over the world. In 1998 he traveled to one of bin Laden's terrorist training camps in Afghanistan. That's where the terrorists planned to start "an operation" in America, he said; they planned to meet in Canada. It might have been nice to put this guy away, huh?

Canadian intelligence was actually looking for Ressam too. But they didn't know about the alias he was using. In 1999 a French investigating magistrate sent Canadian officials a formal request for this terrorist's arrest. The Canadians needed *six months* to process the request.

So our Millennium Bomber stayed a free man until the day he drove his explosives-filled rental car onto U.S. soil. Oh, and did I mention that for years the generous Canadians gave him $500 a month in welfare benefits? Are you kidding me? This is how our neighbors to the north are fighting terrorism?[4]

You and I both know that Ressam's story isn't the only one like this. Nope; this is just the one we caught.

Think maybe we should be paying attention to our border up north?

THE POLITICS OF PETTINESS

So the Canadian situation is bad. In fact, it is much worse than we usually hear. We hear a hell of a lot more about the Mexican border. And actually, that makes sense, because it is a mess. A total mess!

The Mexican border is such a big mess that private citizens felt they had to take it upon themselves to try to do something about it. In April 2005, a group of private citizens formed the Minuteman Project Civil Defense Corps to monitor and alert the U.S. Border Patrol when they witnessed illegal crossings on the U.S.-Mexican border. Since their inception, the Minutemen have brought tremendous public awareness and political pressure to the issue of immigration. Several field agents have credited the volunteers with cutting the flow of illegal aliens into the targeted area. When the Minutemen were patrolling, the number of apprehended illegal aliens dropped from an average of 500 a day to less than 15 a day.

How did the U.S. Border Patrol respond? Did they get on the ball once these citizens drew attention to the problem? Uh, 'fraid not. According to more than a dozen agents in Naco, Arizona, Border Patrol supervisors ordered them *not* to arrest illegal aliens along the twenty-three-mile section of the Arizona border where volunteers patrolled. The Border Patrol didn't want to do anything to show that the Minutemen were effective. "It was clear to everyone here what was being said and why," said one veteran agent. "The apprehensions were not to increase after the Minuteman volunteers left. It was as simple as that."[5] Another agent said the Naco supervisors "were clear in their intention" to keep new arrests to an "absolute minimum" in order to offset the effect of the Minuteman vigil. Again and again, those in charge, those whose job it is to ensure our safety, have taken the low road of politics, arrogance, pettiness, and downright incompetence.

WAKE UP

Since the Minutemen made national news, there have been congressional debates, massive protests, and lots of speeches and TV appearances. There have been plans and programs, bills and amendments. There has been a lot of politics. What there hasn't been is really serious action to actually try to *fix* this problem.

In 2005, Congress passed the National Intelligence Reform Act, which required the hiring of 10,000 Border Patrol agents over the next five years. But the president's budget included funding for only 210 new agents. Both houses of Congress worked together, *twice,* to bypass the president's decision and hire 1,500 new agents—less than the 2,000 required by law, but way better than 210.

Representative Tom Tancredo, chairman of the Congressional Immigration Reform Caucus, hit the nail on the head when he said, "We need to get the president to come to grips with the seriousness of the problem. I know he doesn't like to utter the words, 'I was wrong,' but if we have another incident like September 11 by people who came through our borders without permission, I hope he doesn't have to say 'I'm sorry.'"[6] Damn right! But then Tancredo got it wrong. For all his bluster, instead of getting a bill passed for his president, he stood in the way of the president's attempt to get an aggressive immigration bill passed, supposedly because he was holding out for something tougher. When you see him, ask Congressman Tancredo whose side he's on.

Pay attention, my friends, and please try to understand this. I am not against immigrants, I am against illegal immigrants. They are—how do I say this—*illegal*! How can we possibly consider ourselves safe and secure with millions and millions of unaccounted-for people in this country? We do not know how many are criminals or potential terrorists, and that is unacceptable. We can institute any plan you like, so long as it includes finding those people who came here illegally. I don't care whose plan we use—amnesty, throw them out, keep them, whatever—but for sure, we have to know who is here. Next, we need to stop the bad guys from coming here. Fence it, moat it, use land mines, guards, battleships, or all of the above, but we have to get control of our borders. We should not stop immigration, but we should and must stop *illegal* immigration.

One way to curb the influx of illegal immigrants is to stop those who hire and help hide these illegal immigrants. There is only one way that will work: huge fines or jail time for those caught in the employment of illegals—thousands and then millions of dollars in fines, and then if it happens again, the CEOs of the companies should go to jail. If we are serious about wanting to secure our borders, that is what must happen.

Almost anything would be better than the abject nothingness that is our current immigration policy. Our very brave and capable Border Patrol agents are overwhelmed and underpaid, so they cannot stop the tide. Only Congress can pass the laws that would provide the money necessary, and only the president of the United States can provide the leadership and the courage that this issue demands.

We have taken a step in the right direction—kind of. We've said that we would deploy 6,000 National Guard members to the border between Mexico and the United States. This is about 20,000 too few, and in fact by the summer of 2006 we had managed to deploy only about 900 to 2,500 National Guard people (depending on who you believe). But it is a start nonetheless. These troops monitor surveillance cameras and sensors and build roads and fences, freeing up the Border Patrol agents to actually patrol the border and take people into custody.[7] This would be an even better step if, once we took people into custody, we didn't just let them go.

It used to be that when the people immigration authorities call OTMs—other than Mexicans—were caught crossing the border, they were entitled to a hearing in front of a judge before being deported. Since we didn't have anyplace to put them until that hearing, we let them go with a court date. Guess what? Most never showed up for court (just like the Millennium Bomber in Canada); they simply melted into society and they are probably still out there. In November 2005, Homeland Security chief Michael Chertoff announced that we would end this policy. That's good, but he didn't give us a time line. How quickly we can stop the "catch and release" policy once and for all totally depends on how long it takes us to obtain funding, develop plans, gain approval, and actually build enough detention facilities.[8]

There have been some positive signs, though. In October 2006 the government announced that 186,000 people had been deported for immigration violations since the previous October; that represented a 10 percent increase in deportations from the previous year. Plus the number of illegal immigrants the Border Patrol apprehended dropped by about 100,000.[9] It's a good bet that there's a connection between the two stats: the more illegals we deport, the more people will think twice about trying to sneak into this country. But I can't give the government too much credit on this one. Whatever steps we have taken wouldn't have happened if it hadn't been for groups like the Minutemen and all the attention Americans drew to the immigration issue.

THE VISA PROBLEM

It isn't just all the illegal immigrants we have to worry about; we also need to worry about those people we let into this country legally. Almost all of the 9/11 hijackers obtained visas to come to the United States. This means they filled out their paperwork and were granted permission, by us, to come here. Had we looked closer, or even looked at all, we might have noticed that as many as *fifteen* of them shouldn't have been granted permission to enter our country.[10] According to *National Review*, six experts have agreed that all fifteen application requests they reviewed from government files should have been denied on their face value. Some didn't list a specific destination, which is a requirement on the two-page form. In fact, one of the terrorists listed his destination as

"No." Other applications were incomplete; lines that asked for gender, nationality, and home address were left blank.[11]

While some of these technical problems have been fixed, the underlying philosophical problems regarding immigration have not. In March 2006, as part of an effort to improve relations between the United States and Saudi Arabia, the president approved a program that will allow 6,000 students from Saudi Arabia to study at American universities. The Saudi Ministry of Higher Education and the General Authority of Civil Aviation are offering scholarships to Saudi men and women to study various majors related to civil aviation in the United States. You do remember where the 9/11 hijackers were from, don't you? Yup, most of the guys who hijacked the airplanes were from Saudi Arabia. So while it is a good idea that we talk to this country and try to get them to stop churning out murdering wack jobs, allowing them to learn to fly here again is not something even Allah would think was a smart move.

People come here legally (or, as with the 9/11 hijackers), sorta kinda legally, and then we lose track of them. As of June 2004, millions of people had overstayed their visas and Homeland Security has no meaningful way of tracking them down. This is not surprising because, well, it's Homeland Security, and we know they suck. But we also know some of the 9/11 hijackers stayed here on expired visas. We know this is a tool the terrorists use, and yet we have done nothing—repeat, *nothing*—to remedy this situation.[12]

We have made minimal progress to correct mistakes in the area of student visas. Just so you understand why this particular aspect of alien status is as important as the others, I remind you that at least one of the September 11 hijackers entered the United States on a student visa. This is not nearly as embarrassing as the fact that six months after the 9/11 attacks, the U.S. government issued student visas to two of the hijackers to attend a flight school in Florida.[13] Of course, they didn't need them, since they had died in the act of murdering 3,000 people. Better late than never? This is more than embarrassing, this is massively incompetent; this is a huge "what the fuck" yelled from our highest mountains and on every street corner. This is bullshit!

Students from other countries come here and act as spies for their countries. How's this for a hypothetical? A student from China, attending the Massachusetts Institute of Technology, has access to our entire Internet and to our brightest minds, and he reports everything—and I mean everything—that he learns to his handlers in China. The information is checked, and if the student spy doesn't give good information, his funding is cut off, or his family is threatened, or worse. Guess who teaches at MIT? The former director of Central Intelligence John "I-did-not-have-those-secrets-on-my-computer-but-I-need-a-pardon-anyway" Deutch is a professor of chemistry teaching there. Yeah, I think we want to keep track of the students we let into the United States.

In 2003, the U.S government created the Student and Exchange Visitor Information System (SEVIS), an Internet-based software application that colleges and universities are required to report to so we can track and monitor students here on visas.[14] Congress spent $36.8 million to create the system; most of the costs are supposed to be offset by fees paid by foreign students. It costs around $100 to register. In its first year, it detected more than 36,000 potential violations of student visas nationwide. It sounds pretty good, doesn't it? Of course, then we discovered that only 1,600 of these violations were investigated, and according to the U.S. Bureau of Immigration and Customs Enforcement, which operates the system, agents made 155 arrests as a result. Anyone a little worried about the other 35,000 violations? I sure am.

How about we actually investigate all the violations, not just a small percentage?

As it stands now, we have a pretty open policy on who can come here for a visit. If you are from a country that we consider one of our friends, you don't need a visa; you can just hop on a plane and come here. We need to stop this. Everyone gets a visa from now on. We have homegrown nuts of our own and we don't need anyone else's nuts coming here. We can make rules to allow for frequent business visitors, we can make this a speedy process, but everyone fills out detailed paperwork and gets checked out by our government agencies before they come here.

Either we are going to take this seriously or we aren't. I vote for taking it seriously because the consequences of not doing so are deadly.

HOUSE OF CARDS

When we talk about border security, not only do we need to know who is coming here, we need to know *what* is coming and how it is getting here. We saw in Chapter 4 some of the different scenarios that could play out if terrorists are successful in attacking us again. Given the threats we face, we might want to control the nasty and lethal stuff being brought into our country. But border security is not a simple issue.

Twenty-three million containers enter the United States each year. They come by air, truck, rail, and boat, and they play a large role in our economy. Any disruption in the transport of these materials will have a serious economic impact.[15] Case in point: the West Coast dock strike in 2002 racked up losses of $1 billion per day. It took us weeks to catch up because of the traffic backlog that was created by the ten-day shutdown.[16]

While increased security may slow things down and have a significant impact on our economy and the availability of goods, so would a terrorist attack anywhere in the United States. Specifically, the impact on one of our ports would be significantly debilitating. So securing our borders is a delicate balancing act between safety and economic survival.

Three million containers cross the U.S.-Canadian border yearly at Michigan. Many of these containers carry municipal solid waste from Canada and enter Michigan by truck at three ports: Port Huron,

Detroit, and Sault Ste. Marie. Each month at Port Huron alone, approximately 7,000 to 8,000 containers of waste cross Michigan's border.[17] Currently, U.S. Customs uses X-ray machines to see inside these trucks and containers. Only one problem with this: X-rays of trash containers are usually unreadable. It is close to impossible to tell what is inside a container using X-rays. There could be a nuclear bomb inside one of these containers. We could X-ray the hell out of it and we still wouldn't know it was there.

There is better technology available. Singapore is using it now. For about $7 per container, new technology can photograph the exterior of each box, screen for radioactive material, and collect a gamma-ray image of the contents within each box. This could happen while the container is still on the truck. The truck would continue to move at ten miles per hour and therefore any delay would be minimal. The system allows inspectors to sound the alarm on suspiciously dense objects—like a lead-shielded WMD. Inspectors inside the United States who are trained to spot possible nuclear weapons would then review images of the container's contents remotely.[18]

We can also install sensors inside containers in order to track their movements. General Electric has developed a sensor called Commerce-Guard that can be mounted inside a cargo container and can tell government officers if a container is opened at any time en route from factory to stores. This provides protection during the most vulnerable leg of any container's journey: the trip from the factory abroad to a foreign port. We can do lots of things. All of it takes money and a change in attitude—that is, being serious about our national security. We need to get serious.[19]

Nearly 8 million containers come through our ports each year; of those, only about 6 percent are inspected closely. This leaves us incredibly vulnerable. Not a single, solitary open-water or river port in the United States of America is adequately secured. None! Sea and river ports are difficult but not impossible to secure. Ports cover large open areas and provide many varied ways of entering—the water on which they are based, the land next to the water, and the vast road networks needed to support the port facility. It is a lot of area to cover.

Want to get some idea of how bad this can get and just how vulnerable we are? Let's look at the Port of Tampa. No one expects Florida to be hit. We tend to think that the terrorists are stupid and that they will try to hit D.C. or New York again. But Tampa has a population of 320,000. Tampa is a tourist hub. It is also Florida's busiest port in terms of raw tonnage of cargo. Half of Florida's cargoes include hazardous materials such as anhydrous ammonia, liquid petroleum, gas, and sulfur. Tampa has a nuclear power facility. Tampa is also home to Central Command (CENTCOM) and MacDill Air Force Base, where the wars in Iraq and Afghanistan, and any other place in the Middle East that might have to be conquered or disturbed, are headquartered.[20] Any serious attack on the Port of Tampa will cost us billions in commerce and kill untold numbers of people.

So what have we done to fix this? According to Stephen E. Flynn, national security expert at the Council on Foreign Relations, our government has taken some individual steps, but on the whole port security remains "a house of cards." Among the steps taken:

- The Coast Guard has created new security standards known as the International Ship and Port Facility Code.
- Ships heading to U.S. ports now must provide at least ninety-six hours' notice of their arrival, giving the Coast Guard time to do a pre-arrival security check and/or arrange for an inspection.
- The U.S. Customs and Border Protection Agency, part of the Department of Homeland Security, has required ships to electronically file their cargo manifests at least twenty-four hours before they are loaded overseas. Analysts at the agency's National Targeting Center review the manifests, and suspect ships may be intercepted at sea.
- The United States has gained permission from dozens of foreign

ports to have our customs inspectors search the contents of U.S.-bound ships whose manifests have been flagged by the National Targeting Center.

- U.S. Customs, together with the World Customs Organization in Brussels, has set up new international trade security standards.
- Importers are signing on to the Customs-Trade Partnership Against Terrorism (C-TPAT), agreeing to investigate their own operations and supply chains to improve security where vulnerabilities are discovered.
- The Departments of Defense and Energy have developed programs specifically geared toward detecting "dirty bombs," nuclear weapons, and other WMDs.
- The Energy Department, with its Megaport Initiative, is setting up radiation sensors in major ports around the world. Specially trained U.S. Navy boarding teams may, with permission from the host country, inspect suspect ships.
- The White House has unveiled a National Maritime Security Strategy to "present a comprehensive national effort to promote global economic stability and protect legitimate activities while preventing hostile or illegal acts within the maritime domain."[21]

Of course, none of this has truly helped much. There are too many agencies doing too many things individually without any coordination with each other and without any real budget to get their jobs done. It's a farce to believe we know which containers are suspect or which things need inspecting. Our reliance on other countries and companies to do what they have promised, and therefore inspect the contents of all containers coming into the United States, is not merely misguided but flat-out wrong. They aren't doing it. We know they aren't doing it, and yet we let the stuff in anyway. Here we go again using the *H* word. We are *hoping* today won't be the day we guessed wrong.

THE ONLY ALTERNATIVE

Our premises are all wrong. We are approaching border security in the same way that the CIA is still fighting the War on Terror—with a pre-9/11 mentality. We are using all the assumptions we employ to catch drug dealers and smugglers to try to catch terrorists—and let me tell you, one of these things is not like the other. Terrorists do things differently because their goals are different. For example, terrorists only need to get one nuke through a port; smugglers are looking for a constant way to bring in contraband.

If we keep doing things the old way, we will come to regret it. This is a new kind of war, and we need to adjust our thinking and do it fast.

In February 2006, all hell broke loose when we tried to export some of our port security responsibilities to the United Arab Emirates (UAE). The deal did not go through and there was a lot of arguing back and forth about exactly how much access the UAE would have had to our security information. The bottom line is this: any security information shared with a country that deals with al-Qaeda, boycotts our friends the Israelis, and is one of only three countries that recognizes the Taliban is too much.

The Dubai port deal stank to high heaven. It is not the way we should be doing business. You can't have a government that claims its number one priority is our nation's security and then makes this deal with terrorist supporters. Giving up any part of our security to places like Dubai or China is suicidal and stupid. Simply put: foreign companies should not be allowed to influence the security of an American anything. Now, they can own some ports, and they can get special treatment for providing terrific security on their end, but full disclosure of information and control of a port, train, or ship has to be the responsibility of the United States. Would we have allowed Nazi Germany or imperial Japan access to our ports during World War II? What I am suggesting is that we must of course stay in the world community, but we must also ensure that American companies have absolute control over every aspect of the actual security of the operations of transport.

At no time should our security information reside on a computer in a country other than our own.

Our government has to pay attention to something besides poll numbers and reelection. Having a free society does not mean our society has to be an unsafe one. We can have worldwide commerce and still have security, but again, it will cost money and be painful. So what? The alternative is 9/11 on steroids.

CHAPTER 8

BRAVEST OF THE BRAVE, LED BY IDIOTS

The United States of America's military is the reason we even have a country. The Army, Navy, Marines, Air Force, and Coast Guard—they are the reason we can get up in the morning and do pretty much any goddamned thing we want. They, not their political bosses. Our armed forces are the reason we are respected and, yes, feared throughout the world. It is military men and women who leave their families for months and sometimes years at a time to go to places most of us cannot name or find on a map. They get paid next to nothing and they do all of this to protect our way of life.

It is the soldiers, grunts, truck drivers, medics, mess sergeants, Special Forces, Rangers, and SEALs who make us great. Their bosses, the generals and the "it's all about me" colonels, cause us to lose sight of our goals.

Our guys and gals in the green, blue, white, and camouflage are the ones who endure conditions of living and working that are, in many cases, hell on earth. Sometimes it is life in a jungle or a cave. It is almost always life at or below the poverty line. They do this for one simple reason: love of country.

Want to know what living conditions are like on the Iraqi battlefield? Let's take a look at just a few of the conditions and medical problems this army faces while you sit in that comfy chair in your air-conditioned room with that iced beverage at your fingertips:

- According to my sources on the ground in Iraq, the insurgents and terrorists are resorting more and more to unconventional warfare— extra-judicial killings (EJKs), IEDs, vehicle-borne IEDs, suicide vehicle-borne IEDs, mortars, abductions, and so forth.
- Since the beginning of the Iraq war more than 18,000 U.S. troops have required medical air transport out of Iraq due to disease.[1] The Army doesn't know what diseases we're talking about or why the number is so high. Might be nice to know, don't you think?
- By 2006, more than 850 soldiers in Iraq had been diagnosed with a parasitic skin disease.[2]
- A number of U.S. soldiers in Iraq have died suddenly from unexplained blood clots; some soldiers' families and doctors blame the anthrax or smallpox vaccines.[3]
- Private Zeferino Colunga arrived in Kuwait fighting a 102-degree fever, chest pains, and a swollen spleen. Army medics diagnosed him with tonsillitis. After being airlifted to a hospital in Germany, he contracted pneumonia and died within two days from a 105-degree fever. It appears he got ill after receiving a series of anthrax vaccinations right before he was deployed to the Persian Gulf.[4]
- According to UPI and the *Christian Science Monitor,* just a few months into the Iraq War medical caregivers were so overwhelmed that hundreds of wounded or sick soldiers were being forced to wait weeks in stifling barracks before they could get proper medical attention. One officer said the living conditions were unacceptable.[5]

There are lots more examples, but you get the idea. The most noteworthy aspect of all of these findings is that they are all the product of abominable leadership. No self-respecting leader would allow these things to occur. He or she would investigate and fix the problem, making sure the troops were getting the best of care.

Morale is also a product of this kind of leadership. Psychiatric problems can in many cases arise in soldiers who feel they are on their own without a leader who is concerned about their unit's safety. (The Army reports that nearly 7 percent of all medical evacuations from Iraq and Afghanistan are the result of psychiatric disorders.)[6] Good leadership would not have let this happen. Heads would roll or resignations would be submitted, and the fallout from this travesty would have been heard throughout the land. But it didn't happen. Shame on us!

Our troops deserve better. They have saved the world from the Nazis, imperial Japan, floods, hurricanes, famine, and now terrorism. They have never tried to take over our country like the military does in almost every other country all over this world. They save our lives every day, and yet we rarely know about it. They take an oath and swear to their God to uphold the Constitution.

When soldiers see combat, they are changed forever. But neither the fear nor horror of the fighting would deter them from a repeat performance, even when they know in advance the price they are being asked to pay. They may lose arms, legs, reproductive organs, eyes, ears, or their ability to speak. When they were sent to the hills of Korea and then the jungles of Vietnam, they dug trenches that were literally full of shit—both human and animal—and then they had to get in the trench and sleep in it.

Most recently, we witnessed their awesome power and capabilities during Hurricane Katrina. When the city, state, and federal governments so obviously failed to protect our citizens from disaster, a three-star general, Russel Honore, showed up and said, "We are not stuck on stupid," and he then gave the orders that began to fix things. That is our great military, which is always there. If we are to survive and thrive, they will always need to be close at hand.

The United States of America has billion-dollar satellites and Predator drones. We have great weapons, tanks, trucks, mechanized vehicles, food, computers, communications, and gear. We have the bravest and best soldiers, and clearly these amazing soldiers come from the best country. However, none of this matters at all if we don't have great leaders. We could have the most expensive and best of everything, but without great leaders we would still suck. In Iraq and in the War on Terror, we are rapidly on our way to sucking.

During World War I and World War II, and occasionally in Korea, officers actually fought alongside their men. They led from the front. At that time, they understood that they were fighting for our nation's survival. Our earlier wars were fought over big issues: the assault on our European allies and the growth of a virulent and intolerant nationalism during World War I; the Japanese attack and sinking of a major portion of our fleet at Pearl Harbor; Nazi Germany's attack on and occupation of sovereign European nations and the attempt at the "Final Solution" through the Holocaust. The military hierarchy recognized what these threats entailed and acted like leaders: men like John J. Pershing, George S. Patton, Omar Bradley, and my father.

Toward the end of World War II, we got lazy and stupid. It seems we lost our way, and it is reflected in the other battles we have had to fight: Korea, Vietnam, Grenada, Lebanon, Bosnia, Kosovo, and the failed Iranian hostage rescue. Somewhere along the way, between technological advances and arrogance, we started to believe we could do war without casualties. The officers of the corps lost its sense of purpose by taking on the roles of briefers, writers, and career men; they were no longer soldiers. They did not appear to care about their men, only about themselves and their futures. These are the people in charge today. We can't win the War on Terror with this current crop; nor can we win with the current way of thinking and doing things.

A FEW GOOD MEN

To be fair, no matter how bad it gets, there will always be a few good leaders in the mix. But we need more great leaders like the ones we've had in past wars.

During Korea and Vietnam there were stunning examples of great leaders. John L. Throckmorton was a rare breed in the Army during the Korean War. He liked to fight and he did not run. His bravery and leadership are the stuff of legend. He had begun his career with the First Army in the European Theater during World War II. During the Korean conflict he was the commander of the 5th Regimental Combat Team. He was someone that young soldiers like Lieutenant Hank Emerson remember standing and fighting, killing bad guys, and caring for his men. As a result, when Lieutenant Emerson became Lieutenant Colonel Emerson, he went to Vietnam and remembered what made a good leader. Guess what? He was a brave and caring son of a bitch like Throckmorton. They both led from the front; they fought with their men and they did not run.

Another sterling example of a commendable leader is Colonel David Hackworth. He was given eight Purple Hearts, ten Silver Stars, and two Distinguished Service Crosses. Colonel Hackworth earned each honor he was granted. He had all the values of a true leader, the same ones he wrote about in his book *Steel My Soldiers' Hearts*. The values are courage, perseverance, communication skills, and teamwork. Hackworth had a feel for battle; he loved his men. He was innovative, selfless, and an amazingly brave soldier and leader. He may have been the best of us all.

In Bosnia, we also had a couple of great guys. Bill Carter was the three-star Army general who became the chief of staff for the Bosnian mission. He was brilliant, caring, and trusted by all. Admiral Leighton "Snuffy" Smith Jr. was another outstanding leader. As a Navy attack pilot, he flew 280 missions in Vietnam and received two Distinguished Flying Crosses. He became a four-star admiral and was the director of operations, U.S. European Command J-3. This guy was a risk taker, and he was also brilliant. He is one of the three best leaders I have ever seen, and that is saying something, since I hate all Navy guys except Navy SEALs (who are really not Navy guys but more a product of Special Operations).

Carter and Smith are retired now, but fortunately we still have some great leaders. One is General Jim Jones, a Marine who is the current NATO commander. Another is Colonel Gerry Lauzon, an Army air defense artillery officer who championed the case of "leading by walking around"—kind of like New York's mayor Ed Koch.

Then there is Major General Eldon Bargewell, who is in Iraq now. I'll be honest: I don't like this guy, and he doesn't like me. In fact, if we see each other again, it will probably result in a fight. But there is no doubt about it: he's a great leader. He is extremely brave and smart, and he truly takes care of his soldiers. Back in Vietnam, Eldon got seriously wounded and still saved the day. For his heroism he was awarded one of the nation's highest medals, the Distinguished Service Cross. He has always gone to the sound of the guns; he was the commander of Delta Force, America's premier counterterrorism force. Recently, he has come to the attention of the public as the chief investigator for the alleged atrocities of a Marine unit in Haditha, Iraq. There was no one better qualified to investigate what really happened than this officer, this leader. Eldon left the Army in late 2006; it will be a long time before we see the likes of him again. You want to know about leadership, go ask Eldon Bargewell. I did mention that we don't like each other, didn't I?

All of these truly exceptional leaders have one thing in common—they cared more about the mission and the men than they did for themselves. Each is, or was, exceptionally bright and tireless. Each had an ego big enough to fill a room. Those egos were based on fact; these guys really were the best in the room.

Unfortunately, such leaders are the exception. If they were more common, we would have been out of Iraq and Afghanistan two years ago. We have lost the kind of leadership where officers actually are wounded or killed along with their men. We very rarely see the kind of leadership where men and women will follow you—anywhere, anytime—just to be around you.

THE RISK TAKERS HAVE VANISHED

Signs of great leadership can be found by looking at the soldiers who are being led. How do they fight? How is their morale? How do they care for each other? Great leadership is the glue that binds together those who fight.

When your men and women are driving a truck full of explosive fuel 300 miles into enemy territory and they are being killed, mauled, and torn apart as they drive, you as a leader need to get yourself in a truck and ride with your soldiers. You must share the danger. You do not ever give an order you are not willing to carry out yourself. You may not drive the truck as well as the soldier, nor shoot the gun as well as your marksmen, but you need to show up. You need to take the risk. That is how you lead.

Let me be very, very clear. This kind of leading and risk taking applies to *everyone*. When there is true leadership, lieutenants, captains, majors, lieutenant colonels, colonels, and, you betcha, generals must get their asses into the trucks and the Humvees and share the risk. You need to shit in your pants when the bombs go off, get hurt, and maybe risk getting dead alongside your soldiers. That is what the salute is all about, that is what the order is about, and that is what the officers should be about. If they don't do these things, they are not leaders. The only ones they are kidding or fooling are themselves; their soldiers know better.

What happens when leaders start sharing the danger? We get smarter leaders, smarter orders, and better organization. We do things right instead of doing them wrong. Instead of not shooting looters because it looks bad, we get leaders shooting looters and creating law and order. Instead of trucks not having armor because the Pentagon didn't think ahead, we get armored trucks because leaders start screaming at their bosses.

When leaders who share the danger leave the military and go into government service, they will not have to guess what it is like to be in battle. They will know the awful reality of what is at stake, and because of this, war will always be the last resort. People will get fired, not rewarded, for missing 9/11 and WMDs and for turning Iraq from a glorious victory to the troubled land we see today.

It is true that leadership is difficult to define. One man's great leader is another man's jerk. I say George Patton was a great leader; others say he was a screaming asshole. Some say Douglas MacArthur was a brilliant leader; I say he was a self-serving mama's boy. Some say Norman Schwarzkopf was a great leader; I sure don't. He was brave and brilliant and also one of the most arrogant, overbearing officers ever to put on a uniform. Bill Clinton and others say Wesley "I-let-80-percent-of-the-Serb-army-drive-home-after-I-bombed-them" Clark was a great leader. I say the only difference between Clark and Schwarzkopf is that one is fatter than the other.

Still, even if we can't all agree on the great leaders, we can usually spot the bad ones straightaway. We just have to look at their actual accomplishments and failures, leaving out how many times they were promoted. If we do that with the military leaders in Iraq and the War on Terror, we see right away that we are plagued by bad leadership.

Want a name? How about this one: General Tommy Franks. Franks' job was to face, chase, and kill the enemy. A good leader does this because that is what he has trained his troops to do; he knows his men, and he knows that doing his job involves putting them at risk. You tell them that, and you go with them when and wherever you can. But Franks did not have the courage to put his men at risk to get Osama bin Laden; he refused to send 900 Rangers in to capture the terrorist. He didn't want his easy victory in Afghanistan to be tarnished by a disaster or the loss of life. But taking such risks is what leadership is all about, especially in combat. The general failed and bin Laden got away. Franks sucks as a leader.

Franks is a good example of the huge problem in Afghanistan and Iraq: at almost every turn, those making the decisions have been more concerned with themselves, their careers, and appearances than with the mission or the men and women serving under them. Where are the risk takers? They've usually been pushed out, sent home, or punished.

In 2003, for example, General Eric K. Shinseki, chief of staff of the Army, said that several hundred thousand troops would be needed in postwar Iraq. But the Pentagon brass called Shinseki "wildly off the mark" and said that postwar Iraq would require only 100,000 troops.[7] The Pentagon undercut the Army to make their point. They leaked information on Shinseki, they ridiculed his numbers (which, by the way, the Army staff had produced), and then they announced his successor fifteen months before Shinseki was set to retire, which of course made him a lame duck.

Army Secretary Thomas White was fired in April 2003 after expressing his agreement with Shinseki's assessment of the needed troop levels in Iraq. According to *USA Today*, Defense Secretary Donald Rumsfeld "was furious with White when the Army Secretary agreed with Shinseki." In an interview after leaving the Pentagon, White said that senior Defense officials "are unwilling to come to grips" with the scale of the postwar U.S. obligation in Iraq, adding, "It's almost a question of people not wanting to 'fess up' to the notion that we will be there a long time and they might have to set up a rotation and sustain it for the long term."

For most of his career, Shinseki was competent but nondescript. It was not until the end of his career, not until the moment when he stepped forward as one of very few truth tellers about the number of soldiers needed to sustain our victory in Iraq, that he became a risk taker. He told the truth, and Rumsfeld was so pissed that he moved him out early, did not show up at the retirement ceremony, and hired a guy three years into retirement to take his place. What was the lesson others learned from this? I can tell you what it wasn't—it wasn't to tell the truth to the powers that be.

GETTING IT RIGHT

Good commanders, good soldiers, and good analysts can agree with me when I tell you that the military has been trying to fix itself for years. We want to be sure that we do not repeat our own negative history. One such fixer of the military is H. R. McMaster. Colonel McMaster is the consummate poet-warrior. He was the commander of the 3rd Armored Cavalry Regiment and senior U.S. officer during Operation Restoring Rights, during which we drove terrorists from their stronghold in the city of Tall Afar. As McMaster himself said, the terrorists had waged "the most brutal and murderous campaign against the people of Tall Afar . . . Not only were they targeting civilians, brutally murdering them, torturing them, but they were also kidnapping the youth of the city and brainwashing them and trying to turn them into hate-filled murderers." McMaster's troops worked with Iraqi security forces, and got good intelligence on the terrorists from the people of Tall Afar. In the process they helped win over Iraqis who might have doubted the coalition's intentions.

I've been on a rant about how we haven't been getting it right. McMaster got it right; he used everything in the military toolbox. He fought with his troops and he won the hearts and minds of the people his unit was defending. His troops and the people of Tall Afar had truly become a coalition force.

McMaster gets it. After Operation Restoring Rights, he told the Pentagon press corps, "The American people have got to be so proud of our soldiers. . . . They are tough, they are disciplined, they are compassionate. . . . The American soldier is pursuing the enemies of Iraq, they're pursuing the enemies of our nation. We are committed to this mission to bring freedom and security to 26 million people here. And it is very clear to our soldiers as we go into these areas, as we see these caches, as we see the horrible acts that these people have committed, as we see the extremist literature and the intolerance and the hatred that this enemy possesses, it is very clear to us that these are enemies of our nation, and we are proud to be here to pursue them and defeat them in Tall Afar and broadly throughout this region."[8]

Here's a leader who took the risks necessary to achieve victory. McMaster knew he was putting his troops in harm's way, but he knew that the ultimate goal—driving out the terrorists and not losing the faith of the Iraqi people—demanded strong and resolute action. He also understood, from experience, the kind of sacrifices that he was asking his fighting forces to make, and it was nothing he hadn't done and wouldn't do himself. Tall Afar was a continuation of a career that had demonstrated the kind of leadership we need more of in today's military. McMaster had acquitted himself brilliantly during the Battle of 73 Easting in February 1991, one of the only real gun battles in the first Gulf War outside of the fighting done by the Special Forces.

McMaster knows too that part of being a leader is being up front with the troops and witnessing firsthand the reality of the situation on the ground. While on active duty, he wrote the definitive piece of criticism on the Vietnam War, *Dereliction of Duty*. In this treatise he correctly places blame for the mistakes in Vietnam on the shoulders of the presidents and generals. He shows how generals could, and did, forsake their troops by glossing over what was really happening in the war. He claims this was done in the name of political expediency; they wanted to further their personal careers and reputations. McMaster also states that personal reputations stained by such cowardice cannot stand the test of time and history.

He got it right. It took guts to level such criticism at our leaders' war-making decisions while still serving on active duty. But he didn't get fired for his truth telling. That's because he is a great officer, as he later showed in Iraq. Sure, McMaster's revelations in *Dereliction of Duty* earned him his share of criticism. Some called him a headline seeker; others called him a screamer. I call him the future of the Army. The same goes for new generals like Brigadier General Michael Jones, the assistant division commander for the 1st Cavalry Division in Iraq. He is a fighter; he cares about his men; he is very smart. We can't promote his type fast enough. McMaster, Jones, and a few others may yet save the Army from itself.

Another leader who has dared criticize the civilian leadership and the micromanagement of military operations by civilian authority is Major General John Batiste (U.S. Army, Ret.). General Batiste made headlines in April 2006 by publicly calling for the resignation of Defense Secretary Donald Rumsfeld. General Batiste's most frequent criticisms of Secretary Rumsfeld were with regard to insufficient funds for infrastructure repair and inadequate troop strength. He took particular issue with Rumsfeld for insisting on keeping troop strength low, in spite of the pleas from subordinates. During an interview, Batiste was questioned about McMaster's right to publish his book while still on active duty. Batiste's response was, "I think that the book, *Dereliction of Duty,* is something everyone ought to read. I think Colonel McMaster had every right to write it while he was on active duty. It was some years after the Vietnam War, and I think that's a healthy discourse that we must have."[9]

We need to have a healthy discourse on our present situation as well. It took years for us to even talk about Vietnam and begin to learn the lessons of that war. In fact, it is just now that our officer corps has begun to really study Vietnam. The generals and politicians are the ones who don't want to talk about the mistakes that were made, because they are the ones who made them. While it is usually right to wait until a war is over and then look back at the mistakes we made, this war has gone too wrong for too long. We don't have the luxury of waiting. Every day we refuse to learn from the mistakes we have made, and are making, in Iraq and Afghanistan means more dead soldiers.

WHAT HAPPENED TO RESPONSIBILITY?

We can start our discussion by saying that if you think leadership is just about leading soldiers into battle, giving a snappy salute, and yelling at Marines in boot camp, you are wrong. Do you think leadership doesn't play on the big stage in Washington, D.C.? Do you think a mistake by our leadership "only" kills soldiers? You are wrong again. Only the truly stupid think that. I know you are not among the turnips; you chose to read this book! You are probably brilliant.

What story of our warfare in Iraq has appeared more than sixty times on the front page of the *New York* (Damn) *Times*? What story got the president of the United States to apologize? What story is erroneously synonymous with American cruelty and American embarrassment? I am speaking, of course, of the Abu Ghraib prison story. Certainly the soldiers who treated the prisoners in Saddam's torture chamber in the most juvenile, cruel, stupid, and illegal ways were responsible for their conduct. But so also were their *leaders*. You know who I mean—the people who take the salutes, ride in the right front or right rear seats, have the big rank, and make the big decisions. You know, the bosses!

But what happened to responsibility? The leadership piled it on the backs of those at the pay grade of Private Lynndie England. She became the poster soldier with a picture of her pointing at the private parts of prisoners. Want to know what these brilliant sons of bitches did, these leaders, when they were asked to take responsibility for their soldiers' actions, which is the basic requirement of all who would be in the leadership business? They made a deal; they took the Fifth Amendment; they took immunity; they denied; they avoided.

Nope, it was not Rumsfeld's fault. It was not his policies, nor his lack of preparedness for the victory we had won. No, that had nothing to do with this. Of course not, Lieutenant General Sanchez! You were the ground three-star boss at the time. Nope, you knew nothing. No, Major General Geoff Miller, you took the Fifth when asked to testify for a soldier. A soldier was in need and you took the Fifth! Colonel

Thomas Pappas, the intelligence boss at the time, took immunity! These are not officers; these are not leaders; these are cowards, faux officers, play soldiers, and poor excuses for leaders. Never has this nation, this military, been witness to such low-life, scum-sucking bottom-feeders as this crew.

Even the *Army Times*, which usually reports the party line, felt the need to publish an editorial titled "A Failure of Leadership at the Highest Levels." The editorial began, "Around the halls of the Pentagon, a term of caustic derision has emerged for the enlisted soldiers at the heart of the furor over the Abu Ghraib prison scandal: the six morons who lost the war. Indeed, the damage done to the U.S. military and the nation as a whole by the horrifying photographs of U.S. soldiers abusing Iraqi detainees at the notorious prison is incalculable. But the folks in the Pentagon are talking about the wrong morons. . . . While responsibility begins with the six soldiers facing criminal charges, it extends all the way up the chain of command to the highest reaches of the military hierarchy and its civilian leadership."[10]

Rumsfeld finally got his head chopped off in November 2006. He resigned the day after the elections, when the American people confirmed with their votes what Batiste, six other retired generals, the *Army Times, Navy Times, Air Force Times, Marine Corps Times,* and I had been saying for months, even years. But the commander in chief did not see fit to replace the incompetent Rumsfeld with the kind of risk taker we so desperately need. All the president did was change a face, change the look of things; he did not change the policy. But he did make a speech that "sounded" like a change, and only time will tell if it was more than a speech. Bush appointed a guy named Gates, the former spook and head of the CIA under Bush 41. Besides not knowing the difference between a tank and a parachute, Gates, on his best day, is like watching paint dry. He never makes a decision without checking with his boss, his wife, his dog, or his driver. He is risk averse. It would be hard-pressed for Gates to do any worse than Rumsfeld did, but it is highly unlikely that he will do any better. We need real leaders.

What do I mean by real leaders? Well, for starters, real military leaders would have first made sure that all the soldiers in Iraq, but for this discussion at least those guarding prisoners, were trained. They would have been trained in how to guard prisoners. The key words here are *train* and *guard*. Guards do not interrogate; interrogators interrogate. Leaders would have made sure that guards guarded and interrogators interrogated, and they would have made damn sure everyone was following the rules. They would have supervised their soldiers; they would have checked on them at all hours of the day and night; they would have led by example, *Do as I do. Follow me.*

Unfortunately, there weren't any leaders at Abu Ghraib. So what are the consequences of this lack of leadership? It is a nation embarrassed forever; the Muslim world more pissed at us, as if that were possible; and a prison more infamous than the country in which it is located. So yeah, leadership can have large-scale effects, not just on the battlefield but also on the world as a whole.

THE FALLUJAH FAILURES

When talking about failure of leadership in Iraq, we also have to talk about Fallujah. The name means bad things to all of us. It means the terrorists' stronghold that we bypassed in 2003 when we took Iraq. It means four dead Americans, private security guards, who were ambushed and hanged from a bridge. It means finally deciding to send in a great Marine unit that was kicking some major bad-guy ass, only to be told by incompetent and uncaring men and women seven time zones away, to stop and pull back. Why? Because some Iraqi newspaper and politician said that there were "scores" of dead and wounded civilians showing up in the hospitals around Fallujah. Guess what? Never happened! At the time of the report, there was not a single wounded or dead civilian in all of Iraq that had been caused by an American bullet, let alone the numbers being thrown out that day. It further turned out that insurgents planted the story. So our guys pulled back and out. The terrorists celebrated and dug in some more.

Fallujah means we finally, after meetings, briefings, and conference calls, went into the belly of the beast with serious force, Army, Marines, Special Forces, and the Air Force, and took the town at a cost of at least 42 U.S. troops dead and more than 300 friendly Iraqis killed. Fallujah means we left and put the Iraqi military in charge and then the bad guys came back. Fallujah means an absolute failure of political leadership and some failure on the part of the military.

Let's look at the military failure first. The order to our military to abandon Fallujah while we were winning was an order of such stupidity that I was expecting it to be disobeyed, or at least to see a general or two quit over it. That never happened, so the military has some culpability there. But the real culprits in the Fallujah fiasco are the head guys in Iraq: Paul Bremer, the head of the Coalition Provisional Authority; General John Abizaid, the senior military commander in the area; and Donald Rumsfeld himself. All of them said we were killing innocent civilians, so the attack had to be stopped! I am throwing up again. Did anyone check out the story before we threw away our best chance of making a dent in this war? How about surprising us by not having a knee-jerk reaction? It is exactly this type of leadership that gives me and many others pause, or more correctly, downright depression. It also leads us, those in and out of uniform, to the conclusion that the leadership has a low regard for the soldiers' well-being and the nation's defense.

Here is another example of that lack of leadership. Twenty-four Iraqi civilians were slaughtered by U.S. Marines in the town of Haditha on November 19, 2005. The Americans shot men, women, and children at close range as retribution for the death of a Marine who was killed in a roadside bombing. Marines went from house to house killing members of three families. The girls killed in one of the houses were ages fourteen, ten, five, three, and one. An investigation was ordered after *Time* magazine broke the story, which included accounts of survivors and videotape showing some of the victims at the Haditha hospital and the victims' houses. The home of the victims of one family is marked with graffiti that claims, "Democracy assassinated the family that was here." Al-Qaeda now uses the massacre and videotape of the victims to recruit new members.[11] The Marine Corps relieved Lieutenant Colonel Jeffrey Chessani and two of his company commanders. The alleged cover-up by Kilo Company's superiors is still under investigation, although the military is beginning to prosecute some of the Marines involved.

IN SEARCH OF REAL LEADERS

Want to see poor leadership? Look at the officers who won't go out with their men on patrol. Look at the Green Zone in Baghdad, where you can buy plasma televisions and new cars and hang out at bars and talk tough. Here is a basic rule of combat: when you can sell plasma TVs in a war zone, it is time to come home. Look at the SEAL platoon that sat on its ass for a year because its officers were too afraid to commit them. Look at the SEALs fighting in Afghanistan with their backup more than ninety minutes away by helo. Ninety minutes away is no backup; that's body bag pickup.

Or look at what's happened after the death of Pat Tillman, the NFL star who left behind a lucrative contract to join the Army after 9/11. Ranger Tillman was killed by friendly fire in Afghanistan, in a tragic fog-of-war incident. How can this loss be any worse? It is worse when the U.S. government and the U.S. military lie to the family. It is worse, criminally worse, when after two and a half years and five investigations, the family still doesn't know what happened to their son. It is worse when the military awards a medal to your dead son that the son did not earn and would never have accepted if he were alive.

There are many more examples of bankrupt leadership in Iraq and the War on Terror—too many for just a chapter. The point is that leadership, both political and military, is what our nation sorely lacks right now. Lots of so-called leaders show up when it is a perfect 65 degrees in the shade and all the bad guys have been vanquished. They show up for the press conference or the parade. Leadership is much more difficult when there are bombs going off and soldiers are being mangled and killed, when other nations are abandoning you, when your own press and political party start turning against you. We need leaders who understand the need to protect soldiers from stupid politicians and also protect our way of life from those who wish to destroy it.

We find this kind of leadership in the Special Forces because of their more realistic training, long deployments, and smaller units. As a result, the enlisted and officers create a bond that—when it works—is the envy of the rest of the military. When it is overdone and a friendship develops, it can be detrimental. Special Forces officers get a different and worldlier military education. They are taught to deal with insurgents, ambassadors, spies, and other countries' elite military units. They are expected to be more independent. A regular Army infantry officer (the Special Forces guys call them the Big Army) would never have gotten near a horse, let alone used them as the Special Forces did to capture Afghanistan. These guys are risk takers.

We need leaders who care only for the mission—getting it done and bringing their men and women back in one piece. We need the risk takers, those who will sneak around the corner to get to the enemy, sometimes not even asking the bosses' permission, but getting the job done anyway. Risk takers never call back to the Pentagon for an assignment; they just do their jobs. Risk takers hate meetings; they are too busy killing bad guys.

You find risk takers everywhere but seldom with a lot of rank. We must promote these individuals now. A risk taker would have shot looters in Iraq right from the beginning. A risk taker would have dropped a grenade down that hole where Saddam was hiding. Risk takers are always in trouble with the boss because they tell the boss things the boss does not want to hear. Risk takers sometimes are found disheveled and dirty like their men and women, or cleaning equipment with their unit while the other "officers" are having a drink in the Officers' Club.

Only real leaders and risk takers deserve the soldiers that we visit in Walter Reed Medical Center and Bethesda Naval Hospital. Only real leaders, who know how to take risks, know how to lead those kinds of soldiers. Only real leaders can win this war. We need to go find them, now. If we had real leaders, real risk takers in Afghanistan, bin Laden would be dead by now.

If we had these kinds of leaders, we would have been out of Iraq by now.

CHAPTER 9

HANDS OFF

"I do solemnly swear (or affirm) that I will support and defend the Constitution of the United States against all enemies, foreign and domestic; that I will bear true faith and allegiance to the same; and that I will obey the orders of the President of the United States and the orders of the officers appointed over me, according to the regulations and the Uniform Code of Military Justice. So help me God."

When I became an officer in 1970, I took this oath. Everyone who joins the military takes this oath or a similar one.

I can hear you saying, "Yeah, so?" Well, so this: the oath matters! From reading it, you know that recruits are taught, right from day one, that their first priority is to *defend the Constitution.*

The president also takes his oath to the Constitution: "I do solemnly swear (or affirm) that I will faithfully execute the Office of the President of the United States, and will to the best of my ability, preserve, protect and defend the Constitution of the United States." The vice president takes the same oath as *all* other federal employees: "I do solemnly swear that I will support and defend the Constitution of the United States against all enemies, foreign and domestic, that I will bear true faith and allegiance to the same, that I take this obligation freely, without any mental reservation or purpose of evasion, and I will well and faithfully discharge the duties of the office on which I am about to enter. So help me God."

In all of these oaths the Constitution comes first. It is what we all swear to uphold. It is what we all swear to protect and defend. It is what soldiers die for.

So what does it mean? Why is defending the Constitution such a big deal? I'm not a lawyer (thank God), but I'm an American and I know that all of this matters because the Constitution is the thing that makes our country what it is. The Constitution is the underlying force in our way of life. It separates us from, and raises us above, every other country in the world. It is what makes us free.

The War on Terror shouldn't change that. Sure, during war there are areas where we are going to have some conflicts to resolve, and the *way* we resolve those conflicts matters. The way we decide what we will give up and what we won't matters. The way those in power decide to go about dealing with the delicate balance between security and freedom matters. The way we do this shows us what we will be and what will be left of our way of life when the war is over. So it matters, or it should, to all of us.

Since 9/11, we have heard a lot about civil liberties. Every piece of legislation, every discussion of tactics used in the War on Terror, every story about enemy combatants, detainees, and terror suspects inevitably leads to a discussion of civil liberties. To some critics of our government, practically everything the United States has done since 2001 is appalling, reckless, and a terrible threat to American society. To take such an extreme view is a big mistake; not *everything* is a constitutional crisis, and if our government is going to prevent another 9/11, it does need the tools to catch terrorists. But that's not to say that our government should have carte blanche, that the War on Terror can justify any and all government decisions. We absolutely need to protect our civil liberties, which are the very freedoms our guys in uniform have been protecting over the past two centuries.

Civil liberties have nothing to do with red states or blue states,

Democrats or Republicans. This civil liberties issue is a red-blooded-American issue. This is a why-we-are-who-we-are issue. I am not an elected official, and I'm not nearly smart enough to pretend to understand the deep, hidden meaning the framers of our Constitution intended to convey, but I do know a thing or two about right and wrong. I spent almost thirty years in nameless places, without my family, doing soul-destroying things in the name of protecting our freedoms. I feel qualified to tell those who claim to be bringing freedom to Iraq while they try to trample on my rights, "Hey, asshole, come trample on this, if you can. I got something for you, and so do all the brothers of the cloth who served before me, with me, and since me."

While the ongoing argument about civil liberties might piss us off and make us feel as though we're fighting ourselves at times, it is absolutely 100 percent necessary for us to address these issues. They aren't just important; they are essential.

THE PATRIOT ACT

Right after 9/11, in October 2001, Congress passed the Uniting and Strengthening America by Providing Appropriate Tools Required to Intercept and Obstruct Terrorism Act. Quite a mouthful. That's why we call it the USA Patriot Act. The guiding idea was that in order for the United States to have any possibility of thwarting another terrorist attack, we must be allowed to carry out surveillance on whoever we think may pose a threat to our country. The Patriot Act extends to the fight on terrorism the same tools that have been used for decades to fight organized crime and drug dealers. These tools have been reviewed and approved by the courts. Senator Joe Biden of Delaware explained during the floor debate concerning the act, "The FBI could get a wiretap to investigate the Mafia, but they could not get one to investigate terrorists. To put it bluntly, that was crazy! What's good for the mob should be good for terrorists."[1] I am not endorsing anyone here, but this guy makes sense on this particular issue.

Some good, commonsense things came from the Patriot Act; in fact, we need some of the provisions in it—or at least variations on them—to fight the War on Terror. But the truth is that, on the whole, the Patriot Act was, and still is, a massive and inexcusable mistake. It undermines our citizens' civil liberties without any real need to do so. The basic concept was a great idea—but not the authoritarian way in which it can be and is being enforced.

The Patriot Act allows the federal government and local police departments to write their own warrants without oversight from any judicial authority. They can also seize information about you and not tell you they've done it. First off, law enforcement should not have the ability to write its own warrants. We have a system of checks and balances to protect the individual from the power of the state. To ensure that the police or the FBI or other law enforcement agencies don't abuse their power, they have to go before a judge and request a warrant showing that they have probable cause. When you do away with the judicial check, citizens are in danger.

The Patriot Act gives the government even more power by making it a crime for anyone to tell that he or she was the recipient of one of these self-written warrants. The person can go to jail for up to five years just for telling someone—a lawyer, a judge—this happened. The Patriot Act leaves citizens without a way to fight the power of the government.

Although the act was written to help us combat terrorism, the government is using it in every area of law enforcement. The FBI has actually used the Patriot Act to go after owners of a strip club as well as in cases of bribery, money laundering, computer fraud, copyright infringement, child pornography, and all kinds of other things. The Bureau has served over 120,000 of these self-written warrants, and most people whose records have been seized don't even know it.[2] Using these methods to fight terrorists is one thing; using them in normal criminal proceedings against citizens is a definite no-go. How do you feel knowing that the same government that missed 9/11, missed the WMDs in Iraq, and totally screwed the pooch reacting to Katrina now has your records? Scary, isn't it?

This is not how the government is supposed to behave. This is not what we are all about. We are about openness and accountability. Doing all of this in secret, when it isn't necessary, breeds suspicion and makes it understandable that our own people don't trust their government anymore.

MISTAKES WERE MADE

There have been some checks on the Patriot Act and on the government's surveillance power.

In September 2004, a federal court struck down a Patriot Act provision that allowed the FBI and other executive agencies the power to obtain information about anyone at all by issuing so-called national security letters. National security letters had been created in the 1970s and represented a narrow exception to privacy rules because they allowed the FBI to secretly get business records on a person suspected of being a terrorist or spy. But now the FBI said everyone's business was up for grabs under the Patriot Act—no warrants or other judicial approval necessary.[3] The federal court disagreed. It ruled that the Bureau could not use the Patriot Act to get customers' records from Internet service providers. The court also said that the law's gag provision—any company ordered to give over a person's records couldn't tell the individual—represented an "unconstitutional prior restraint of speech." The court actually used the words "democracy abhors undue secrecy."[4] It probably won't shock you to hear that the government appealed that decision.

The National Security Agency has been conducting an eavesdropping program since shortly after 9/11 without the warrants required under the Constitution. The administration calls it the Terrorist Surveillance Program. I call it crap. Oh, I think eavesdropping on terrorists is a great idea—a necessity. But the way we are doing this, without warrants, stinks and is illegal.

There were provisions that already existed within the law for these kinds of situations. There was a super-secret court created by the Foreign Intelligence Surveillance Act of 1978. The FISA court was available to the government—at any time—to go over the evidence to determine whether there was probable cause to eavesdrop. If you thought there were not enough judges available to do the work in a timely fashion, you thought wrong. The number of FISA court judges was increased from seven to eleven in 2001 upon the passage of the Patriot Act, and no fewer than three must reside within twenty miles of the District of Columbia. I am betting you think doing a wiretap or bugging someone does not happen fast enough. Well, that's not true. It takes hours and sometimes days to do it right; it must be checked and rechecked. So the good guys have plenty of time to get the FISA court's approval. Plenty of time.

The FISA court also had a pretty good track record as far as this stuff was concerned. Hell, when compared to other government institutions or programs like the Department of Homeland Security, it attains superstar status. According to statistics compiled from the Department of Justice, the FISA court did not reject a single warrant application from its beginning in 1979 through 2002. In 2003 it rejected only four applications. Count them, one, two, three, four. Four, *quatro*. That's all. In 2004, the number of applications rejected was *zero*. Seems like this administration was getting almost everything it asked for, so why all the secrecy?

I don't mean that the government should have taken out advertisements in the *New York Times* to tell the American people and the terrorists what we were doing. But why were government agencies subverting the process by keeping this from the FISA court and not fully briefing the appropriate members of Congress? True, the head of the National Security Agency did brief members of Congress in 2003, but clearly not all of them were satisfied with the information they received. One senator wrote a letter to Vice President Cheney right after the meeting saying he didn't have enough information "to fully evaluate, much less endorse these [surveillance] activities."[5] Oh, and for the record, not a single FISA application was ever leaked—which means that these great judges (like my friend Judge Andrew Napolitano, who was a FISA judge and helped educate me on the finer points of law for this chapter) can keep a secret.

FISA even had an emergency provision that allowed the eavesdropping to be done for seventy-two hours without a warrant. With all of these things in place, there was no need for the government to secretly subvert all of these checks and balances and go it alone.

The law used to prohibit this kind of information from being used in a criminal prosecution because we were aware that it might not measure up to normal legal requirements. We know that to protect ourselves we need to be able to listen to what the bad guys are saying and search their stuff to find out what they are plotting, but we didn't want to deny citizens their rights—so we drew a line. We could use this stuff to find out about and disrupt the bad guys from killing us, but we couldn't prosecute Joe Average for the illegal cable hookup that we discovered because we were listening to him talk to his buddy.

We can carry out this fight within the law, and if we can't, we can change the law. Congress has voted in favor of every single piece of legislation that the president has said he needs to fight the War on Terror. This time he didn't even ask. He didn't ask Congress to extend the number of days we could legally eavesdrop before getting a warrant. If seventy-two hours wasn't enough time, how about we give them ten days? No? How about fourteen days? Who would have voted against that? No one.

The FBI has admitted to knowing of at least fifteen al-Qaeda cells here inside the United States of America. That is clearly fifteen too many. So going after them might mean doing nasty things to mosques, like bugging the piss out of them, paying holy men to rat out their flock, and tapping entire communities' phone lines. But how can we sit still knowing that al-Qaeda is here after what happened on 9/11 and what we see happening every damn day in Iraq? We can't, and everyone knows it. It is in our best interest for the government to foster a sense of cooperation, not continue this go-it-alone attitude.

Once the public became aware of the National Security Agency surveillance program, the president had to go before the American people and explain himself and his policy three times. Why? Because some people believe he didn't tell us the truth the first time; either he lied or he was misinformed because his people lied to him. Either way, it is a bad deal for us. Every time we have to stop and explain what we are not doing, or clarify the previous statement, or amend the explanation that we don't spy on Americans (well, just a few Americans—but only overseas . . . well, okay, we really do spy on Americans, but their civil liberties are protected), we hurt the effort. We damage our credibility and we lose the support of our friends and our citizens.

We need everyone in this fight. We need everyone having confidence in us and in the way we are fighting this war. We need those who may not agree with the policy at least trusting us enough to cooperate. We need information; we need public support; we need people to take risks with their careers. People—hell, other governments—will not do that for a government they do not trust. You cannot fight a war with more than 60 percent of your population against you. Well, you can, but not very well. You need to lead them. Sometimes leadership is displayed by admitting you have made mistakes, admitting you need help.

ABLE DANGER

A few years ago, the Pentagon actually got it right and founded a secret unit called Able Danger.[6] This unit brought together the best military operators, intelligence officers, technicians, and planners from the Special Operations Command, the Army, and the Defense Intelligence Agency to focus on al-Qaeda. Their goal was to discover information about al-Qaeda and then use that information to prepare intelligence and military operations designed to detect, monitor, and—when the timing was right—destroy al-Qaeda.

Able Danger worked, at least kinda sorta. Using data mining of mostly unclassified data, they identified 9/11 hijacker Mohamed Atta a year before the attacks occurred. They also detected the al-Qaeda threat to the USS *Cole* in the port of Yemen days before the attack was carried out. We were successful in finding the information; we then failed miserably in doing anything with it.

The guys who found this info said, "Hey, we need to tell the FBI and have these guys picked up." The Pentagon lawyers said, "No!" Then they ordered the information destroyed. Why? Well, because of the big wall that separated foreign intelligence gathering from domestic intel gathering. And because these agencies didn't like to share.

Former FBI director Louis Freeh has told us that the Bureau could have prevented 9/11 if it had been given this information. We had information that could have saved 3,000 lives, and not only did we not act on it, we destroyed it. Lost to us now are the profiles and methodologies used to identify Atta. They are all gone. Why? Petty bureaucratic turf wars and the lack of interagency cooperation and coordination created this mess.

When this unit's success began to leak to the press, our government tried to discredit and ruin the careers of the very competent and brave men who worked on Able Danger. If it were not for Congressman Curt Weldon and a big-time radio guy named Jerry Doyle, they might have succeeded then. Congressman Weldon, who is a little bit of a wacky maverick with good intentions, brought this issue before the public. He and his source, Lieutenant Colonel Anthony Shaffer, who worked on Able Danger, are the reason we know that the government dropped the ball and did not act on Able Danger's information. Shaffer went to the 9/11 Commission and told all about Able Danger, twice. Miraculously, this information was deemed irrelevant; it never made it into the commission's report. Even after the 9/11 attacks, those charged with figuring out what happened were caught hiding from the truth. Doyle, a radio talk show host out of Nevada, interviewed Weldon and Shaffer and got this story out to the American public. The recent reports have called into question some of these claims, but for my money, the idea is terrific.

I understand why there are concerns about operations like these. Having the government sort through our grocery store purchases or pharmacy bills is reminiscent of Big Brother. This makes us uncomfortable. I understand that. But there are ways to protect our privacy and still allow these kinds of operations to be effective. We have policies in place that allow this kind of information to be used *only* when it comes to terrorist activities and *not* for other kinds of criminal prosecutions. We also have in place other safeguards like oversight committees within Congress. Whatever is needed to make sure that the government doesn't overstep its bounds can and should be put in place. What we can't do is ignore a tool that works. Had we acted on the information produced by Able Danger, we might have prevented 9/11. We need to use this tool to help us prevent the next one.

Sometimes these data-mining programs will come up with very private or embarrassing information on the powerful and the rich and famous; Able Danger did. That is one of the reasons that Able Danger is not being used today. However, programs like those in Able Danger never use this information. Another reason Able Danger isn't in use is that some people in power are afraid that a small group of smart, aggressive men and women could put certain intelligence agencies out of business. Actually, I don't think that sounds like such a bad idea!

THANKS FOR COMING; NOW YOU CAN GO HOME

The constitutional protections for citizens shouldn't change. Laws might be expanded and certain things streamlined, but the basic guarantees afforded to us by the Constitution cannot change. The best way to deal with domestic terrorists is still through the court system, as we did with Timothy McVeigh.

But there's another element to all this: foreigners, visitors, and legal and illegal aliens should *not* be afforded the same rights and protections as citizens.

The Supreme Court has historically recognized that our laws apply to all people in this country. We need to change that. We need to have two sets of laws—one for citizens and one for non-citizens. Non-citizens should not have the same protections that U.S. citizens have. There has to be a reward for being a citizen. One reward should be that you don't have your civil liberties trashed. But if you are not a citizen and act like an idiot, or worse, a terrorist, then even if you came to the USA for a better life, you go back to the country you left.

This treatment should be spelled out and known to all before they come here. A list of dos and don'ts for the international visitor should be supplied to all those entering our country. If, for example, you are a religious leader spewing anti-American talk to your flock and you are a guest in this country, you get to go home. Religious freedom while we are at war is only for U.S. citizens—Shinto, Buddhists, Christians, Jews, Muslims, and others. Why? Because we are in the middle of a religious war; fanatical Muslims are using God as a weapon against us, and that is wrong. We can stop it, and we should. So if you are visiting from somewhere else, better be on your best behavior.

The British learned all about this in July 2005 when bombs exploded in their trains and buses. The Brits learned that it wasn't a great idea to let people come from other countries, live on the dole, and spend all their time in mosques and surfing Web sites that preach hatred of the West. They learned that it isn't a great idea to allow and protect, under law, the right to advocate the killing of Western infidels, and then recruit people and plan to do that killing. It took suicide bombers to show them the error of their previously tolerant ways.

Prime Minister Tony Blair instituted a new policy stating that if you come from another country and preach sedition and advocate acts of terrorism, you have to leave. You get sent home. They throw you in a holding cell where you can do very little damage and then they deport your ass. Of course, the courts there have not upheld these policies, saying they conflicted with the Human Rights Act of 1998. But the idea is a good one, and it is one we should use and are using under the provisions of the Intelligence Reform and Terrorism Prevention Act of 2004. This act allows us to deport foreign-born individuals without charge or trial. You preach violence, you leave. You advocate killing us in the public square, you go home. You associate with terrorists, you can leave; in fact, we will help you leave on a slow tramp steamer with lots of work to do on the voyage home. Things have changed. The terrorists are on our soil. We have to protect ourselves. Will the courts here uphold these policies? We'll see, but so far, so good.

Once you are a citizen of this great country, naturalized or not, then you are 100 percent pure United States of America. I don't want to hear any of this "well, you weren't born here" crap. You get all the rights, all the privileges, and all the responsibility that goes along with it. You get everything. Some bad people will take advantage of this. Tough shit! This is the price we pay, and we will get the abusive bad guys and prosecute them. The foreign-born take an oath; they put their right hand up and swear:

> I hereby declare, on oath, that I absolutely and entirely renounce and abjure all allegiance and fidelity to any foreign prince, potentate, state or sovereignty, of whom or which I have heretofore been a subject or citizen; that I will support and defend the Constitution and laws of the United States of America against all enemies, foreign and domestic; that I will bear true faith and allegiance to the same; that I will bear arms on behalf of the United States when required by the law; that I will perform noncombatant service in the armed forces of the United States when required by the law; that I will perform work of national importance under civilian direction when required by the law; and that I take this obligation freely without any mental reservation or purpose of evasion; so help me God.[7]

Welcome aboard! You just took an oath to the Constitution too.

MISTAKES AND DISTRACTIONS

Probably the scariest tool in the government's constitutionally questionable arsenal is the ability to designate someone as an enemy combatant. For the record, *enemy combatant* is a term coined in a U.S.

Supreme Court decision from 1943. It was used to try German spies as war criminals.

Here in the United States, a U.S. citizen cannot be put in prison without being charged with a crime. The exception to this law is when the president decides to declare the individual an enemy combatant. Jose Padilla was designated an enemy combatant and put in prison.[8] Padilla had met with al-Qaeda operatives and on his return trip to the United States was arrested in Chicago. Padilla's lawyer filed a petition in New York; two days later, Padilla was secretly moved to a prison in South Carolina. Since Padilla was now in South Carolina, the New York court where he had been charged no longer had jurisdiction over the case. Of course, Padilla's attorney had no way of knowing this since the government wouldn't tell anyone where he was being held. At the last minute, right before Padilla's case was supposed to go to the Supreme Court, the government indicted him on criminal charges in Miami.

The Lackawanna Six were six Arab Americans, five of whom were born here. The U.S. government tried to charge the six with *listening* to Osama bin Laden, since these guys had been in Afghanistan in the spring of 2001. When the U.S. District Court said that listening wasn't a crime and that the government couldn't charge them, our government threatened these six guys with enemy combatant status. They pled guilty and went to jail for long terms in order to avoid the status. They knew that once declared enemy combatants, they would no longer be able to avail themselves of the U.S. judicial system.

Yaser Hamdi is a U.S. citizen who was born in the United States to Saudi parents and later moved to Saudi Arabia with his family. In 2001 he was captured in Afghanistan and jailed at Guantanamo. This was the first time in American history that a citizen has been stripped of his citizenship and deported without ever having been charged with a crime. Hamdi challenged his imprisonment all the way up to the U.S. Supreme Court, which ruled against the government. The court held that Hamdi was entitled to have the government file charges against him and that he was entitled to a lawyer. Rather than do that, we let him go. We let him go even though the government had said he was so dangerous to national security that we couldn't let him talk to a lawyer.

John Walker Lindh, who was captured in Afghanistan, was a white American who had converted to Islam, joined the Taliban, and enlisted in bin Laden's forces against American troops. Like Hamdi, he was captured in Afghanistan in 2001. But unlike Hamdi, he was indicted, formally charged with terrorism, consorting with al-Qaeda, and attempting to kill Americans. This pathetic young man was given legal representation, and at trial he knowingly and willingly pled guilty. He went to jail.[9] Nice job; the system works. *This* is the way to deal with American citizens. Enemy combatant status should be reserved for noncitizens. To do otherwise opens the door for the government to abuse its power and its citizens.

In June 2006, the Supreme Court handed down its decision in the case of *Hamdi v. Rumsfeld*. This was a big case, and the government lost. The court ruled that the president had overreached in declaring that we would use military commissions to adjudicate aliens who were charged with terrorism-related activities. The Court said that the president did not have the power to do this.

Let's begin with a few assumptions:

1. We are a nation of laws.
2. We are a great people.
3. We for sure should know right from wrong without legal interpretation.

We should have known that holding people indefinitely wasn't going to fly. We should have known that when we put someone on trial, even someone we believed to be a terrorist, we couldn't try him in a secret proceeding where the accused and his lawyer didn't get to hear the evidence against him and couldn't call witnesses, and where anyone testifying didn't have to take an oath and swear to tell the truth. We should have known that setting up a system where there was no checks or balances was wrong.

Again, the way we did this has been a huge distraction. Five years after some of the prisoners were sent to Guantanamo, the Supreme Court kicked the president's teeth in and said, "You are wrong, Mr. President." This was not a good-news story for our side, and it didn't have to be this way.

We should have decided at the *beginning* of the War on Terror how we would wage this war, and how we would do it under our existing laws. We needed a plan. But once again we were caught without one, and it cost us. Now what? We *still* don't know what to do with the bad guys we picked up.

The government has responded to the *Hamdi* decision by passing the Military Commissions Act of 2006, which sets up a system of military trials for suspected terrorists. Of course, we aren't sure how this will work in practice, or even if the courts will rule that it's constitutional. It'll probably take years before we know any of this. The bottom line is that we're still not dealing with the issue.

Let's decide now how to handle this question of civil liberties and get on with the business of killing terrorists.

THE TORTURE QUESTION

No discussion of civil liberties as it relates to the War on Terror is complete until you have looked at the standard to which we hold our military guys and women. There has been a lot of talk about what the standards are, or should be, and very little direction to our people who have to carry out the actual day-to-day application of these decisions. Rules have been issued, then amended, then rescinded, and then issued again. Training has been close to nonexistent or done with a wink and a nod. This has to stop.

We can only expect our military to act like disciplined warriors if they are told what that means and are trained so that they know the rules of behavior. So far, we haven't done that. In a perfect world, everyone would be treated well and the rules and laws governing this treatment would be clear. But there's no such thing as a perfect war, and for damn sure, there are no perfect laws when dealing with terrorists.

The bottom line is that the Geneva Conventions apply to uniformed soldiers from a country that has signed the agreement and agreed to abide by the articles of the Conventions. Terrorists operate outside the law and thus should be treated outside the law. The Conventions do not apply to them—period.

I'm going to go out on a limb here. Torture is clearly a bad, harmful, hurtful thing. It obviously hurts those being tortured, but not so well understood or acknowledged is the fact that it destroys the soul of the one doing the torture. Torture is bad for all concerned—terrible, sometimes. That said, sometimes torture can be a tool to serve the greater good. In fact, there will be times when we *must* use this tool. If we capture someone we know has information that could stop the next 9/11, a Mohamed Atta or an Osama bin Laden himself, torture his ass! This is the classic example of "good men, trying to do good, must know and be willing to do bad things."

I am not advocating giving our forces free rein. Remember earlier where I told you that guards should guard and interrogators should interrogate? Well, here is where that comes into play. We need to train people on how to conduct the most severe interrogations. We can never kill or permanently maim anyone, we should always have a competent medical authority nearby to assist, and there must be some form of oversight to prevent this type of program from being misused.

Look what can happen when you don't have these kinds of safeguards in place. In 2004, the military began court-martials of several U.S. service members deployed to Iraq. The charges were that they had mistreated prisoners and detainees at Abu Ghraib prison. Private First Class Lynndie England was the most obvious. But you can't just blame this on a few misguided soldiers, even though we haven't seen a single senior officer face a court-martial for Abu Ghraib. After England's conviction, she insisted that military commanders were fully aware of what was going on in Iraq's infamous jail. Several investigations into the abuse have disclosed that CIA operatives worked at Abu Ghraib alongside U.S. military intelligence personnel who were trying to obtain useful information.

Abu Ghraib was wrong because American soldiers are never allowed to treat prisoners in the manner we all witnessed, however silly it looked in the infamous pictures. We don't treat people this way. We are a nation of laws; our soldiers are honorable men. We are not the terrorists. We need either to kill these guys on the battlefield or, if we don't, to be prepared to treat them in accordance with the laws that govern military behavior. Trained interrogators should be able to walk right up to the line with the bad guys. They should not have to treat these prisoners with kid gloves; we should be able to be tough on them. What we shouldn't do is allow military guys with no training to go anywhere near the line. That is not their job.

Abu Ghraib was also wrong because it distracted us. Did you enjoy the Abu Ghraib scandal? The *New York Times* had a field day, and as I said before, featured Abu Ghraib sixty times on the front page. We must avoid this type of distraction, and the way we do that is to let the light in—let's talk about the rules *before* the scandal occurs. The president and his appointed officials, people like the attorney general and the secretary of defense, should get out front, talk about torture, talk about the treatment of prisoners, talk about the ugly things. This does two things: first, it lets the bad guys know we are really nasty people they don't want to screw with; second, and just as important, it lets the American people get ready for the mistakes we are bound to make.

The War on Terror is not like any war we have ever had to fight in the past. Therefore, the rules, the discussion, and the reactions have to be different. Unless we talk about how far we are willing to go to preserve our way of life, we'll be reading about it on the front page of the *New York Times* and spending a lot of time apologizing when we should be fighting. Oh, wait! We already did that. How about we try to not do it again?

The rules governing treatment of prisoners are also not clear, and even if they were, we haven't trained our soldiers in how to treat prisoners properly. We have these untrained guys in charge of this kind of stuff, and the results have been predictably bad. General Geoffrey Miller spent his whole life dedicated to being a field artillery officer until he was put in charge of Gitmo, and then he became part of the command structure at Abu Ghraib. Miller knew squat about running a prison, and we got what we deserved for having an untrained senior officer in charge of something as sensitive as keeping terrorists in prisons.

On June 11, 2006, three high-national-security-risk terrorists at Gitmo hanged themselves. Some might say that's a good thing—three fewer terrorists. It might be, or it might not be. If they were bad guys, then it is merely three fewer we have to guard. If they were just in the wrong place at the wrong time—if we picked them up just because they were in the way or because one of the Afghan tribes handed them over when we were paying for bad guys—then we screwed up. Military incompetence, poor training, and godawful leadership were demonstrated one more time.

We have to get a handle on this stuff. These mistakes are killing us.

We have ways of making laws in this country, so let's make some. Let's have a real conversation about what's needed to fight and win the War on Terror, and then we can put Congress to work deciding which rights we really have and how this war should proceed. Let's not leave these decisions up to the administration and the intelligence community to make behind closed doors. We need to shine a light on this process because I, for one, don't trust them to do this the right way unless it is done with oversight. Do you trust them—the same men and women who missed 9/11, missed tons of WMDs, and turned a military victory into a full-blown insurgency? I don't want these people patting me on the head and saying, "Trust me." Nope, not me! No way! Nohow! Too many good men and women have died and continue to die.

In order for this to work, the American people need to get engaged, pay attention, and tell Congress what they want done. We need to threaten Congress with their jobs if they don't do it right. It's the only way some of these pantywaist, do-nothing congressmen will deal with these complex issues and speak out about constitutional protections. When do these people start to care? When it's their own ass on the line.

Look what happened when the FBI raided the office of Congressman William Jefferson. Suddenly, when one of their own was threatened, congressmen of both parties were screaming about overreaching executive powers. Oh, sure, *now* they want to yell and complain. *Now* they care about separation of powers.

FIGHTING THIS WAR RIGHT

I will say it again. Things are different now. Times have changed. The bad guys are here. We need to use all the weapons in our arsenal. But before we allow the government to touch our rights, before we are asked to adjust our mind-set and let the government into places where it is usually forbidden, a few things must happen. The most important of these things is for the government to start fighting this war right.

The intelligence community and the people who they report to must get their heads out of their asses and begin to get this stuff done and done right. My reason for being so harsh is that in 2006 we witnessed the third change at the top of the CIA. Every new CIA director means a complete change in all head positions, like in collection and spying. So our senior intelligence service is spending more time moving the chairs around and changing the seating arrangements than spying on bad guys. The CIA needs to hire and train hundreds of qualified individuals who speak the language of the terrorists, and we need to start with Arabic. The agency must recruit foreign nationals to infiltrate al-Qaeda in order to guarantee that al-Qaeda really starts to suffer.

The military has to get some real leadership at the top—people who know how to fight and are willing to care more about their soldiers than politics. We need leaders who will tell the truth—leadership that will win this war. We need generals who will ride in the same trucks as their men. We need generals who do not take the Fifth Amendment when asked to testify for their soldiers about policies that they implemented and that their soldiers carried out, even if the policies were wrong from "jump street."

Our government must start taking this war seriously and must bring terrorist states like Syria, Iran, and North Korea to heel. We can do this by forcing them to stop supporting terrorism.

We need to have our government start talking straight about the religious aspects of this war and exactly who is trying to kill us. We need to have our elected and appointed officials grow a pair! When they stop looking after their careers first and us second, they will earn back my trust. When all this happens, then I might be in the mood to talk about the government expanding its powers and leaning on my individual liberties for a time.

When my government starts to take this war seriously and fight to win, when they start using the tools they already have, then they can have some of my civil liberties—but not for very long. They can have them just long enough to win the war. Then I'm coming after my rights, and anyone who tells me I can't have them back will fight a war with me.

I want us all to be informed, to care, to read, to listen, to question, and to get involved. If you don't, companies like AT&T will give them your phone numbers and call lists. If you don't, we're just going to get more bureaucracy, more incompetence, more intelligence agencies overlapping one another. And government becomes bigger and dumber. Maybe that would be okay in peace, but it is definitely not okay in war.

CHAPTER 10

WHAT CAN WE DO?

Over the years, Americans have learned to be blissfully ignorant of things that don't appear to directly affect us on a daily basis. We are incredibly capable of not paying attention to things that go on in other parts of the world. We have become creatures so consumed with our own lives that when a bomb goes off in India and kills people who don't look, dress, or talk like us, we barely stop to notice.

But we can't get away with that anymore. Just as we aren't fighting the war our fathers fought, we don't live in the same kind of world or even the same country as that of our fathers. Because of the advent of technology and the new global economy, the world has become much smaller. Whatever happens in some far-off corner of the international scene affects our lives right here in the United States. We need to become aware of this and realize that we are truly part of an international or global community.

We need to alter our mind-set and accept, understand, and act like we are in a war for our very survival. If we do this, we will come to realize that the things we do and say, the way we vote, and who is in charge really matters. This realization will bring us much further down the road to winning this war than we are right now. This task is never easy; taking charge of your own destiny and getting involved is tough stuff. But let's examine the alternative: al-Qaeda wins and we're all praying five times a day to Mecca. We are at war; we need to behave like it.

So what do we do? Getting our public officials to make the right decisions regarding terrorism, security, immigration, and all the rest is critical. But it isn't all we can or should do. Here are a few things that all of us can do as individuals that will prepare us for the long fight ahead and will also contribute to victory.

Be brave

The first thing we can do is be brave. The fear generated by this war is the fear of being attacked and the fear of altering our self-serving way of life. That is what drives complacency in America. We think that if we don't pay attention to the bad stuff that is happening, maybe it will go away. It's not going anywhere! So how about from this day forward, one of the things we do is look this war and the bad guys straight in the eye and not blink? When we are unflinching in our resolve, we will not let self-serving politicians or Pentagon officials off the hook.

Being brave means we must look at things as they truly are and not as we would like them to be. It means being strong enough to tell the truth, and accept that truth even though it might be painful. It means being strong enough to tell the truth even though it might offend some group's or organization's sensibilities. There can be no political correctness allowed in this war.

We witnessed the outcry for political correctness when Danish cartoonists drew some pretty funny pictures of the prophet Muhammad. My favorite was the one with the bomb under his turban and fire coming out of his hair. The Arab world went nuts! They were rioting in the streets as far away as Afghanistan, Syria, and India. There were fire-bombings because somebody made a joke. The Arab world publishes pictures of the beheadings of Americans and all sorts of vile crap about our presidents and our flag, and they go all weak-legged over a cartoon? Come on! But still we caved in. Initially, no major media outlet

would print the cartoons. The U.S. State Department actua
need to issue the following statement:

> We all fully recognize and respect freedom of the press and ex-
> pression but it must be coupled with press responsibility. Incit-
> ing religious or ethnic hatreds in this manner is not acceptable.
> We call for tolerance and respect for all communities and for
> their religious beliefs and practices.

This is political correctness on steroids, or said in plain English, *bullshit*! If we cave in to the Muslim world because they get their shorts in a knot over a bunch of cartoons, then we'll cave in when it truly mat- ters and all hope for winning this war will be lost.

Being brave also means we must face up and admit to our mistakes. We have made plenty of mistakes and we will make plenty more. How about we get over ourselves, stop playing gotcha, and start forcing the terrorists to make the mistakes instead? When we make a mistake, the secretary of defense, a general, or even the president should just flat-out admit it and say we have learned from it; then we move on.

When soldiers make terrible mistakes, like they did in Haditha, denying them, justifying them, or excusing them—because the "bad guys are worse than us"—isn't helpful. We are the leaders of the free world. We have moral authority. We are better than the bad guys. We hold ourselves to our own standards, not theirs. There is plenty of room for understanding how things like this can happen, but there is no denying that it's wrong. Being brave means that we need to be able to deal with this, accept it, and promise not to repeat it. Being brave means neither side of the political aisle takes advantage of this kind of tragedy. We must give the benefit of the doubt to our soldiers, but if they do wrong, being brave means holding not just them but also their leaders accountable.

Being brave means that when a policy isn't working, we shouldn't be afraid to say so and make a change. We can't be sidetracked by politicians trying to feed us crap on a stick. Change is not the enemy;

being paralyzed by an entrenched position is. If we stick to a plan that isn't working, it's just as bad as not fighting at all.

Finally, being brave means that we should be willing to sacrifice some things. Do you want our soldiers to have the right equipment to protect themselves and kill the terrorists? Yeah? Then maybe we should make sure our military has the financing it needs. Does that mean we pay higher taxes? Maybe, but so be it. The burdens of this war are falling on the backs of our military and our military alone. It is way past time that we help to carry the load. Or how about our dependence on foreign oil? Could we all contribute to helping with that issue? You bet. Look around—there are things that you can do to sacrifice. For some of our fellow citizens, it has been to sit in the hot sun along the Arizona border to call attention to an issue that truly affects our safety. Ask yourself, *What can I do?*

There's nothing brave about sitting on the sidelines and letting others carry the load.

Be smart

The next thing we can do is be smart.

Being smart means being informed. Remember, "we the people" are in charge, and we need to push our leaders. So we must understand what's going on. That's not always easy. This war is constantly changing. Pay attention. Watch the news. Read the newspaper—read five different papers. Learn as much as you can about what is going on in the world.

Understand that we are at war not with a country but with the Muslim world—or at least part of it. Anything that affects the Muslim world will affect this war, like the cartoons in Denmark or the goings-on in Israel. We can't be limited in our understanding to just the things that happen directly in this war. We need to get smarter than we have ever been to truly understand this war.

Being smart means that we don't always accept what we are told. When Secretary of Defense Donald Rumsfeld was called on the carpet because our soldiers went to war without the stuff they needed—like armored Humvees and bulletproof vests—he said, "You go to war with the army you have, not the army you want."[1] It didn't have to be that way.

Our leaders knew that we were going to war in Iraq at least eighteen months before we deployed. The White House knew, the Pentagon knew, and the intelligence community knew. They all knew it and did nothing to prepare for this eventuality. In an eighteen-month period we could have issued every soldier the correct flak jacket, and for sure we could have outfitted every single Humvee that was going into the fight with the necessary armor plating. We could have given the National Guard and the Reserves gear as good as their active duty counterparts. There are zero excuses for us not having done this.

Being smart also means that you can identify bullshit when you hear it.

Be patriotic

The next thing we need to do is to be patriotic. We have talked about how it's okay to sometimes be on America's team. The truth is that it is truly *necessary* to be on America's team. You can start by being patriotic.

Being patriotic means that we should make sure we praise our soldiers. It means we need to thank them for their hard and dangerous work and say how wonderful they are *before* we criticize a policy. We've already had one war where we took out our frustration with government policy on our soldiers, and it broke this country in places that are still not fixed. You know I'm talking about Vietnam; let's not do that again. Our guys are the greatest and they do this job so that you don't have to. We need to show them our support, even if it means going a little bit overboard. We should make sure that we support the troops and make every effort when we are criticizing government policy that it is never about criticizing the troops.

Being patriotic means not being embarrassed to say thank you to a soldier when and wherever you see one.

Being patriotic means standing up for your rights, the same rights that the soldier you just thanked was or is fighting to preserve.

Being patriotic means sharing in the burden. We need more people in the military. We need the best and the brightest. We are so strapped for troops that the Army has lowered its recruitment standards. It now inducts more recruits without high school diplomas and more youth scoring in the lowest category of the Army's aptitude test, so-called Category IV recruits.[2] Every single time our military lowers its standards on anything, from enlistment requirements to buying weapons to training, bad things happen. Combat is the ultimate challenge, and under the worst conditions it takes the best of us to do it in such a way that you maintain some humanity on the other end. When you lower the standards on something this important, something gives: discipline, operations, consistency, leadership. It happens in every war, every time. You add this to four years and multiple combat tours with the stress on the soldiers, their families—hell, the entire country—and something breaks. It's usually the soldier.

Do you realize that in cities all over this country, high schools are banning military recruiters from talking to students? Parents are refusing to allow their children to *hear* what a career in the military has to offer. This is outrageous.

We've talked a lot about our constitutionally protected rights; well, those rights come with responsibilities. The United States will always need a military. We will always need to be able to defend ourselves. We will always have allies who depend on our help, and there will always be people in faraway places in need of protection, and America will have to answer the call.

In order to do that, we need a strong and smart military. For too long, military service has been looked down upon as someone else's job. We can't do that any longer. We need volunteers from every part of American life. It is wrong for parents to say, "Let someone else's kid go—not mine."

It's time we teach our children that military service is a noble and honorable profession, because it is. It's time to instill in the next generation a sense of duty and obligation—to our country and each other. Our kids are not stupid; they get it. Let them listen. Encourage service. Instill pride.

It will take a united nation to beat this enemy.

Accept necessary changes

The next thing you can do is be willing to change with the times. Be willing to adapt to the changes 9/11 has brought to our country, our policies, and our lifestyle. Things are never going to be exactly the same again. Accept it. Be willing to make certain accommodations.

Dropping your pants and taking off your shoes is the price you pay for getting on an airplane. These things aren't a violation of your rights; you have a choice. Don't want to submit? Then don't fly! You still have choices and rights, but the rest of us have rights as well. As the T-shirt says, "I do not consent to being blown up."

That said, if you insist that I consent to a cavity search each and every time I fly, I demand you profile Abdul Bad Guy every damn time on every plane that flies, period.

Profiling isn't about race or religion or any of those things; it is about identifying those who are trying to kill us. Grandmothers, three-year-olds, and Scandinavian men are not the people we are looking for. The people who flew planes into our buildings and who have launched a religious war against us are young Muslim men who are mostly from Saudi Arabia. It makes sense that we should be looking at them, doesn't it? So be willing to accept this.

Be willing to accept bag checks on the subway. Again, you don't have to submit, but if you don't, you can't ride. As we've discussed, our close friends the Israelis have come close to developing a profile on the suicide bomber. We know how the suicide bomber looks, walks, smells, and sweats. By the way, for the record, that is called profiling. But in our country, even if we came up with the profile, we couldn't use it. New York City gets close to this. For example, when they believe there is a threat, they stop people with bags in subway stations. They might stop you for wearing a long coat on a hot day, at least until the ACLU sues them. But at least Gotham is trying!

The government can and should put cameras on every street corner, on every bus, in every bathroom . . . well, forget the bathrooms, but you get my point. We need cameras and devices to detect things that would harm us. Though cameras alone will not stop a terrorist attack (just ask London, which might be the most surveilled city in the world), they are essential to the fight. They can make catching bad guys easier and could certainly help us manage the consequences if we are hit with a terrorist attack. The mayor of Chicago had it right when he said in the fall of 2006 that he wanted to get cameras on "almost every block" of his city.[3] I know the idea of this kind of surveillance scares you, but every day very bad men supported by very bad countries are thinking of new ways to kill us. You think 9/11 was bad? The next one, and there will be a next one, will be worse. They always are because the terrorists learn from their mistakes as well as their successes. We need to do the same. In order to fight this fight properly, we must be willing to accept some minor inconveniences, or moments of embarrassment, if they protect us and our families and neighbors, and be willing to really inconvenience Abdul Bad Guy like dead inconvenience.

Give of ourselves

The next thing we need to do is give of ourselves. Our soldiers are far from home, in the middle of a hell where people shoot at them. They are giving up the amenities of American society and sacrificing for us every day. Give of yourself. Send them a letter. Say thank you. Send them a care package. Send food, books, movies, and music. Send calling cards so they can call home and talk to their families who are also sacrificing and giving up things for us. Work with your local schools and community organizations to adopt a soldier or a unit of soldiers. Make sure they know that we appreciate what they're doing.

GETTING THE GOVERNMENT TO DO ITS JOB

The things we've talked about so far are personal attitude adjustments. They are the immediate, take-control, make-a-choice things you can do as an individual. But there are some things we haven't previously mentioned that our government can do and in many cases *must* do. It is our job to make sure the government does them.

If we really want to stop terrorist infiltrators from coming into Iraq, we must be willing to use very aggressive, deadly, and at times questionable tactics. Snipers and tanks are only part of the answer. We must change course and get this done. We can do this. We know how; we just need to start fighting this war smart. We can start being smart by asking and answering the necessary questions, like "Who the hell is Ed Brody?"

Ed Brody spent over thirty years fighting our nation's wars as a Special Forces noncommissioned officer. NCO Ed Brody teaches at the Special Forces School at Fort Bragg, North Carolina. He is the most knowledgeable man on the planet about insurgencies and guerilla warfare. He should have an office next to the president, but he doesn't. He should be the guy in charge of this war, but he isn't. Actually, he hasn't even received an e-mail or phone call from any decision maker, planner, or spy in our entire government. Not one person in our government has asked Brody about what tactics would ensure victory, even though everyone who understands how to fight insurgencies knows that Ed Brody is the go-to guy if you really want to win.

Brody is sitting at Mott Lake, a special place in the soul of all Special Forces soldiers, giving the best classes in the world; but no one is taking full advantage of this guy's exceptional skill and experience in the War on Terror.

In November 2005, the chairman of the Joint Chiefs of Staff told us that things in Iraq were going okay because "between the increase in armor and the changes in tactics, techniques, and procedures that we've employed, the number of [IED] attacks . . . that have been effective has gone down, and the number of casualties per effective attack has gone down." He neglected to point out that the number of IED attacks had doubled from 2004 to 2005 and so the overall number of fatalities hadn't fallen.[4] So basically he was saying, *Don't worry that more Americans are being killed by IEDs; fewer Americans are being killed per incident—it's just that there are more incidents.* This is a guy who badly needs to meet Ed Brody. How hard is it to pick up the damn phone and say to the best in the business, "Ed, this is General Flathead. What do you think we should do?"

If not now, when? When instead of more than 3,000 dead we have 20,000 dead? When there are no tricks left in the bag of political spin, someone who knows better will finally call Ed to help us get out of a colossal disaster, but by then it will probably be too late. Someone needs to call Brody now! Write your senator and congressman and ask them why no one has talked to Ed Brody.

Here's another thing our government must do: come up with a workable budget that takes our military needs into consideration. Today, we have 500 aerial refueling tankers that desperately need replacing. Some of the tankers are from the Eisenhower era, for God's sake, and their average age is forty-six. And yet no contract has been signed to replace them.

Since the War on Terror began, there have been 7,000 rescues of military personnel from hostile environments using helicopters. The Air Force wanted to replace its aging search-and-rescue helicopters, but the Pentagon delayed the replacement effort for years. Instead of replacing the helicopters, the Defense Department decided to review and study the issue.

These things and others like them happened because the Pentagon was being run by an over-the-hill bureaucrat whose best days, like many of ours, were forty years behind him. You can't run a war without weapons, and you had best keep them up to date, or when you finally have to pay the piper, your cash flow won't allow the purchase. That is where we are now.

Yet the government has taken some steps in the right direction.

When the White House unveiled its 2007 budget, it called for a 15 percent increase in the number of Special Forces.[5] So by the year 2011, we'd have 66,000 of these guys. That's a terrific start, because these are the main forces that will win this War on Terror.

The White House's budget also called for a major financial investment to purchase new weapons for attacks against terrorists and insurgents and to finally gather the intelligence we need to be successful. But I'm not convinced that all the new military goodies will find their way to the troops. I also have to wonder why the budget called for a 20 percent increase in funding for the Star Wars program, since it hasn't worked once. I think it might be better to take the $2.5 billion and throw it down a well and make a wish.

In 2006, the U.S. Marines commissioned yet another study, this one on helmets. Why do we need another study? We already know what the problem is. And we know the solution too. A nonprofit charitable organization named Operation Helmet reports: "The helmets currently in use by the Marines as well as those projected for the future are engineered to protect against 'ballistics' (bullets) and have only fair protection from blast forces and fragment impacts from IEDs and other types of newly appreciated combat dangers." An estimated 50 percent of all combat injuries are blast injuries resulting in traumatic brain injury; that's a 30 percent increase in traumatic brain injury from other wars.[6] So could we get our guys better helmets to protect them against such blasts? You bet. But they're probably hard to find and ridiculously expensive, right? Uh, guess again. According to Operation Helmet, the necessary shock-absorbing helmet pads are commercially available. And they cost under $100![7]

The Marines say that they can't afford to retrofit the helmets issued to the guys fighting in Iraq and Afghanistan. It seems to me that they can't afford not to.

In the 2006 midterm elections, the people voiced their concerns about Iraq with their votes. The question is: Did our government hear them?

The answer is, regrettably, no. The government's response after more than 25,000 fathers, brothers, mothers, and sisters had been killed or wounded? Typical—commissions, meetings, counter-commissions, and more meetings. There was the plan from the Baker-Hamilton Commission, the plan from Chairman of the Joint Chiefs "Perfect" Peter Pace, and, of course, the plan from the newly empowered Democrats.

On January 10, 2007, the president, in a prime-time speech, gave us yet another plan for success in Iraq. It basically said we are sending 20,000 plus more soldiers into Iraq and we've instituted some nebulous time table for the Iraqi government. As of this writing, the jury is still out, but for sure this is the president's last shot to save a policy that is his alone and is failing.

The speech followed weeks of the political equivalent of rearranging deck chairs on the Titanic. The entire team leading or rather, not leading, in Iraq has been canned, reshuffled, moved around, fired, lessened, or made to retire. From the political leadership in Iraq, with the change of Ambassador Kalaziaid, to the head military guy in Iraq, General Casey, to General Abazaid, the CENTCOM boss, to Mr. Negroponte, the first and so far the worst National Intelligence Director, all have been changed.

None of this will help. Success in Iraq, which I continue to hope for but increasingly see as lost, rests with a political and economic success, as it has for the past three years. Changing a few generals and an ambassador without drastic policy changes will not work.

My bottom line is no more soldiers should die in Iraq. No more soldiers should lose their body parts for a country and a people that will not stand up for themselves. On a recent visit to Iraq, I was once again shown how great our servicemen and women are, how brave, how dedicated, and how they have given enough. Our great military did their job. Now, it is beyond time for our politicians to do the same.

THE HUNT DOCTRINE

Our government needs to do a lot more to ensure victory. But you and I know that there are a lot of things the private sector can do a hell of a lot better than Washington can. Look at what Operation Helmet is doing. The organization was founded in 2004 by a former Navy doctor who wanted to make sure his grandson in Iraq had the right helmet pad to protect against explosive blasts. By October 2006, the organization had sent more than 27,000 of the proper helmet kits to Marines fighting in Iraq and in Afghanistan.[8]

Or look at the work being done by a PR firm called the Rendon Group. In any war, and especially in this war, the propaganda part is key to the fight. A lot of people don't think about this element of the fight, but it must be a vital part of our overall strategy to win the war. We're talking real long-term hearts-and-minds stuff. This is where the Rendon Group comes in. The government has given the organization a multimillion-dollar contract to feed propaganda to Iraq and other enemies. In fact, even before the *first* Gulf War John Rendon was working to try to advance the concept of regime change in Iraq. He worked with Iraqis to form resistance or opposition groups; he helped spread the message through newspapers, television, and radio that Saddam Hussein is a bad guy; he funneled U.S. money to groups that support our agenda; and he planted disinformation in Iraqi news stories.[9]

This is super-secret, on-the-edge stuff. And a lot of people don't like it; some think John Rendon is part of the conspiracy that got us into the war in Iraq—that he is like the Robert DeNiro character in the film *Wag the Dog*. Well you know what? I do like it. We should do more of it, in fact. As I said, hearts-and-minds operations like these are essential to winning the War on Terror. It's not a well-kept secret that our government sucks at these types of operations and most of the time hires them out. I don't care who does the work, as long as it's effective.

Such programs make a difference everywhere, not just in Iraq. Rick Rendon, John's younger brother and also part of the Rendon Group, runs Empower Peace, a campaign that brings young people in the Middle East in contact with American kids through videoconferencing technology. I know what you're thinking: *Not another bunch of tree-hugging, Birkenstock-wearing liberals saying, "Can't we all just get along?"* But that's not what this project is or does. Empower Peace works with the next generation to help Muslims and non-Muslims understand one another—and it works! Although it might be contrary to your nature, we must support these hug-a-Muslim programs. Changing hearts and minds now means we will have fewer terrorists to kill later.

So that's all good. We can point to hard examples of the private sector stepping up to the plate. Still, the sad truth is that we aren't using the civilian community in this war nearly enough. That's a huge mistake when you consider that the United States has the best legal, financial, political, and creative minds in the world. We have the best colleges in the world; let's use them. We have the best fund-raisers and moneymen in the world; let's use them. We have the best public relations firms in the world; let's use them. We have thousands of retired intelligence, military, and police officers who have more experience fighting against an insurgency than the entire crop of current government workers; let's use them. We need help; that help is right in front of us.

This is why I have a simple rule: *if you can't find it in the government, go to the civilian sector and fast-forward it to the combat zone.* Let's start following this rule, immediately.

At the beginning of this book I said we were going to try some common sense. My rule is just common sense. So are my other rules. These are what I like to call the Hunt Doctrine. We've had enough BS and poor leadership and political backbiting and all the rest. It's time for some common sense in this fight. It's time to invoke the Hunt Doctrine.

So here goes, the Hunt Doctrine:

- No soldier shall ever use, fly in, sit on, or ride in any vehicle or weapon that is older than he is.
- Only competent—that means *proven* competent—combat leaders get to lead soldiers in combat.
- When you are in a fight . . . *kill them all.*
- Never ask permission in combat.
- Never commit a soldier to combat you are not willing and capable of supporting 100 percent with everything he needs.
- Never give an order or mission you are not willing to do yourself.

- Always go with your men into the fight.
- As long as you care only about your soldiers and the mission, you can do anything.
- Once committed, the government tells only the truth to the American people when soldiers are in combat.
- Admit when you are wrong.
- It's intelligence, stupid; without it you die.
- The Air Force never runs a war.
- Never care who gets credit, just get it done.
- Love your soldiers enough to hurt them in training.
- Make training harder than combat.
- Make people do their jobs.
- When our troops fuck up, punish and move on.
- Hold the highest accountable, just like the lowest.
- Keeping the peace is always harder than winning the war.
- When the order is stupid, say so, and don't obey it.
- Your boss is only your boss; he is not always right.
- Administrative courage (standing up to the boss, telling the truth to the powerful) is more difficult than physical courage.

Rules to live by. Let's make sure our leaders get the message.

IT'S YOUR CHOICE

All of us, when we bother to think hard about the War on Terror, understand what's at stake. If we don't get involved in this war, if we don't insist on getting it right, if we don't defend the republic against the Islamo-fascists, then all that we hold dear will be lost. Our way of life, our existence, is at stake. The terrorists will not stop. They will not just decide to go away. They must be *made* to go away. They must be killed, and those countries that support them must be dealt with so that they will never do this again.

We understand the stakes, but so far at least, our actions haven't shown that we're 100 percent committed to protecting everything that's important to us. I've shown you the things we can do. We can make sure our leaders are on the ball—and make sure they follow the Hunt Doctrine! And we can sure as hell hold them accountable when they let us down. Yes, we can even complain about failed leadership in this war—it would be unpatriotic *not* to care enough to speak up about our safety and our freedoms—but for damn sure the first thing you should say before leveling any complaint about the war is, "The soldiers are doing great." We can also pitch in, either on our own or by teaming up with others in our community to help out. We each have something to give, some way to help. We can't sit on the sidelines, not with our children's lives at stake.

Yeah, it's not easy—not for our military, not for our political leaders, and not for any of us. There is nothing easy about this war, but for sure there is no quit in us. Stay angry, stay involved, stay informed—or learn to pray on a rug. It's your choice.

THE THREATS—AND HOW WE'RE FIGHTING THEM

Wherever I go, people who recognize me from Fox News ask me, "Colonel, where do we stand in the War on Terror?" The hard truth is that the War on Terror is not going all that well. Without a doubt we've had some incredible successes in this war, thanks mainly to our brave troops. And it's also true that the War on Terror is a struggle that can't be won in just a few years, but will in fact take decades. But the fact remains that we've missed too many opportunities to cripple our enemies, we've let political correctness hamstring us, and, basically, we've gotten complacent.

But it's hard to be complacent when you realize that our enemies are focused on one thing—*killing us*. In the pages that follow you'll see some clear indications of how serious the threats really are, from Afghanistan to Iraq to our very own country. You'll also get an idea of how we've failed to contain these threats.

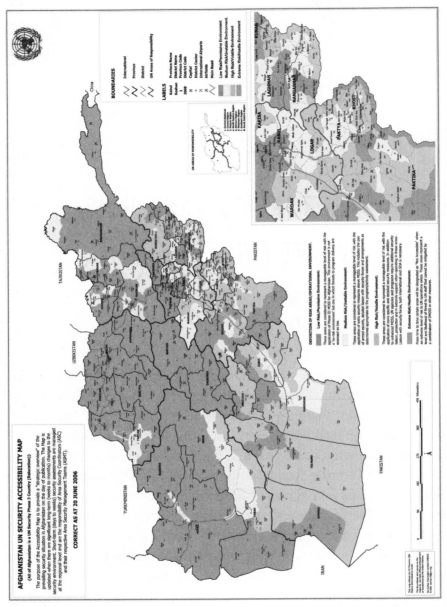

Afghanistan: We kicked ass there, right? Sure, but then we didn't have a plan to keep the peace. So the Taliban came back with a vengeance and the whole southern part of Afghanistan slipped out of our control, as this United Nations map reveals.

Afghanistan opium poppy cultivation increases to a record level of 165,000 hectares

The area under opium poppy cultivation in Afghanistan increased by 59% from 104,000 hectares in 2005 to 165,000 hectares in 2006. This increase is in line with the findings of the Rapid Assessment Survey implemented in January-February 2006 (UNODC, *Rapid Assessment Report,* March 2006).

As a result of the upsurge in opium poppy cultivation in Afghanistan in 2006, global opium poppy cultivation rose by some 33% in 2006 to 201,900 hectares[2]. The share of Afghanistan increased from 62% in 2005 to 82% in 2006.

Figure 1: Afghanistan opium poppy cultivation, 1994-2006 (hectares)

1994	1995	1996	1997	1998	1999	2000	2001	2002	2003	2004	2005	2006
71,000	54,000	57,000	58,000	64,000	91,000	82,000	8,000	74,000	80,000	131,000	104,000	165,000

Figure 2: Afghanistan: Opium poppy cultivation from 1986 to 2006 (hectares)

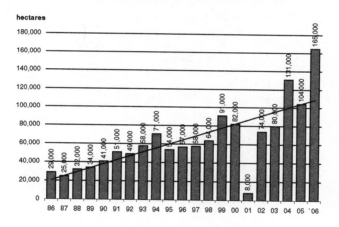

---

[2] Based on preliminary opium cultivation estimates for Myanmar and the "rest of the world".

To understand how things have fallen apart in Afghanistan, look at how that country's opium cultivation and production has skyrocketed since we launched military operations there in 2001. This chart from a report by the United Nations Office on Drugs and Crime tells the story.

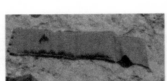

Left - Exterior View of Iraqi Suicide Vest Found in Baghdad. Right: Cutaway Showing Packages which Contain Main Explosive Charge and Ball Bearings for Fragmentation.

Firing Device with Lanyard Port, Two Toggle Switches, and 9V Battery.

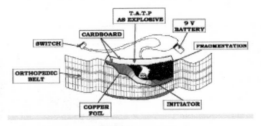

Suicide Vest Used by the LTTE – duel electric firing system, military grade explosives, ball bearings

2

Suicide bombings have become one of the favorite tools of terrorists all over the world. These illustrations, included in a bulletin issued by the Department of Homeland Security and the FBI, show the inexpensive, easy-to-conceal, deadly explosive devices the bombers rely on.

Explosively Formed Projectiles

We are being Targeted

"We are being targeted." That's how the Defense Intelligence Agency began this report on explosively formed projectiles (EFPs). These amazingly simple, devastatingly powerful weapons blow holes in heavily armored vehicles. Oh, yeah, and Iran is supplying them to terrorists in Iraq.

v The Explosive Formed Penetrator (EFP) (shape charge) is
   becoming an Improvised Explosive Device (IED) that poses an
   extremely serious threat to armored vehicles used in Iraq by both
   the military (HUMVEE"S) and Security Companies (Up armored
   SUV's).

v The EFP is a high tech device that has been deployed using
   Passive Infrared Radar (PIR) Devices much like garage door
   openers. Usually the device is observed and then remotely
   activated when a target passes by. The routes traveled by the
   military and PSD teams can be placed under surveillance for a
   given period of time by AIF to determine any patterns developed
   or the device can simply be placed along known routes and
   employed against targets of opportunity.

v Devices are generally used in areas where natural slow down
   points exist, interchanges, steep curves, traffic circles, etc..

v **These devices are well manufactured by experienced bomb makers and then employed by various AIF elements. The following instructions were translated from the an original Arabic Version after having been recovered with a cache of these devices.**

θ **Speed 40 – 60 km**
θ **Height 1m**
θ **Range 4-15 m**
θ **Direction Sideways (refers to angle of attack.**

Background

v Military – class warhead

v Designed to defeat light and medium armour

v Pioneered by Lebanese Hezbollah.

v It is assessed that insurgents have the capability to manufacture these devices.

v The UK has accused Iran of providing these devices to insurgents in Iraq.

Improvised Explosively Formed Projectile
Typical of devices deployed in Iraq

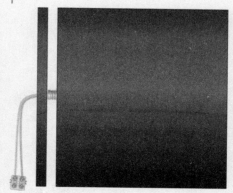 

Device Construction

Constructed from 6 to 9 inch diameter steel pipe, one end of which is sealed with a welded steel plate drilled in the centre to take a blasting cap.

The weapon is filled with high explosive and an inwardly dished steel or copper plate is fitted to the front of the weapon.

It is this plate that is formed into the projectile when hit by the detonating wave from the explosive.

Improvised Explosively Formed Projectile
Typical of devices deployed in Iraq

Formation of the Projectile

The heat and shock wave from the detonation of the explosive projects the steel / copper plate from the front of the weapon at a velocity approaching 2000 metres / second forming a metallic dart capable of penetrating armour plate up to 10 centimetres thick or more at a range of 100 metres or more.

This relatively simply constructed weapon is highly directional and capable of being aimed to a fair degree of accuracy – hence it's popularity as a stand-off anti armour weapon with Islamic insurgents.

Damage caused by a Platter Charge on a Up-Armored HMMWV.

Actual Armor Penetration

Damage to an Up Armored SUV Hit by an EFP

Common Emplacement Techniques

- v Recently we have seen the main charge placed on the curb along side the road and angled upward.
- v Additionally they have been placed on top of guardrails.
- v Usually, but not always, these IEDs are placed on the left side of the road in order to target the vehicle's driver

The EFP Device was offset from the road and concealed in the cement footing of the fence line.

TTP OF ENCASING EXPLOSIVELY FORMED PROJECTILES (EFP) IN FOAM

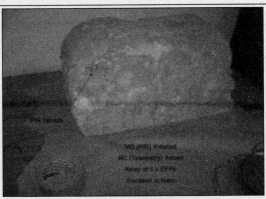

• The entire Passive IR Sensor / EFP device is packaged inside foam and carefully camouflaged to blend in with the area where the device is to be emplaced.
• Recent devices have been colored gray to match concrete blocks.
• The device can be emplaced in a very short period of time (< 2 minutes).
• Once armed, any movement of a person or vehicle in the field of view of the sensor will cause the device to function.
• Unit actions on this type of device are no different to any other type of IED.
• If units have thermal vision recommend they use it to scan areas of known EFP activity (especially curbs, near overpasses and ramps in those areas) to look for object that present different thermal signatures from other objects in the area.

EFPs Initiated by PIR

v EFPs initiated by PIR are designed to defeat armored vehicles fitted with ECM.

v The Triggerman arms the PIR motion sensor by RC. The RC receiver is located outside the protective ECM bubble and is connected to the PIR sensor by CW.

v The EFPs are initiated by the PIR when the target vehicle enters the kill zone.

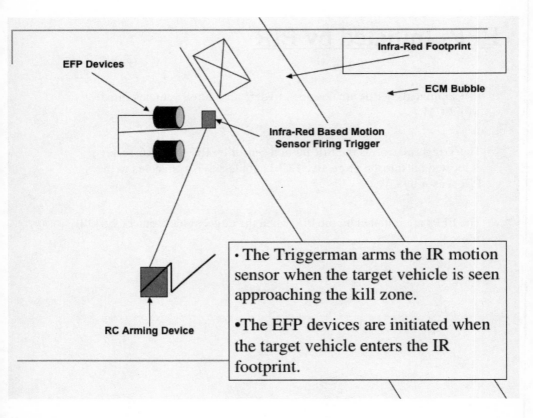

EFP Devices

Infra-Red Footprint

ECM Bubble

Infra-Red Based Motion
Sensor Firing Trigger

RC Arming Device

• The Triggerman arms the IR motion sensor when the target vehicle is seen approaching the kill zone.

•The EFP devices are initiated when the target vehicle enters the IR footprint.

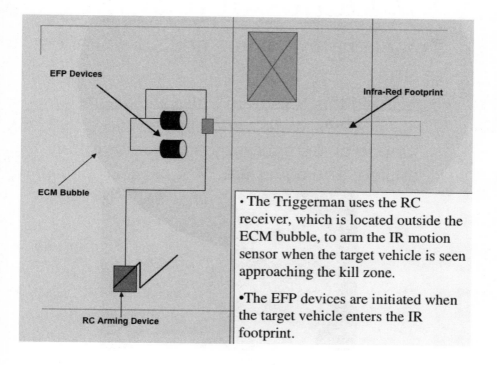

EFP Devices

Infra-Red Footprint

ECM Bubble

RC Arming Device

• The Triggerman uses the RC receiver, which is located outside the ECM bubble, to arm the IR motion sensor when the target vehicle is seen approaching the kill zone.

•The EFP devices are initiated when the target vehicle enters the IR footprint.

7 Duties of a Sniper

1. Target enemy snipers and surveillance teams

- learned this lesson in Fallujah, where *mujahideen* were handicapped more by U.S. Marine snipers than by air raids or other artillery and cover fire.

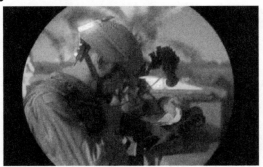

The Defense Department distributed a terrorist training manual to U.S. commanders in Iraq in order to detail the techniques the Iraqi insurgents use to kill Americans. The excerpts shown here reveal in chilling detail how lethal and cold-blooded our enemies are.

7 Duties of a Sniper

2. Target commanders, officers, and pilots, "that is to target the head of the snake and then handicap the command of the enemy."

   - the replacement of officers and commanders is expensive for the enemy, since it may take two to four years and cost "more than $500,000" to put someone through "the famous West Point college."

7 Duties of a Sniper

3. Assist teams of *mujahideen* infantry with suppressive fire. These groups may include RPG brigades or surveillance teams.

7 Duties of a Sniper

4. Target U.S Special Forces.

- "they are very stupid because they have a 'Rambo complex', thinking that they are the best in the world; don't be arrogant like them."

7 Duties of a Sniper

5. Engage specialty targets like communications officers to prevent calls for reinforcements. Likewise, tank crews, artillery crews, engineers, doctors, and chaplains should be fair targets.

    - a tank driver was shot while crossing a bridge, resulting in the tank rolling off the bridge and killing the rest of the crew.
    - Killing doctors and chaplains is suggested as a means of psychological warfare.

 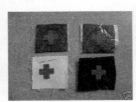 

7 Duties of a Sniper

6. Take care when targeting one or two U.S. Soldiers or [Iraqi] agents on a roadside.

   - "a team of American snipers [may be] waiting for you. They [may be] waiting for you to kill one of those agents and then they will know your location and they will kill you."

7 Duties of a Sniper

7. In the event of urban warfare, work from high areas and assist infantry with surrounding the enemy, attacking target instruments and lines of sight on large enemy vehicles, and directing mortar and rocket fire to front-line enemy positions.

Who would you shoot?
A training exercise.

- Examine the next few pictures and decide who would you shoot first and why.

If you had only one shot, who should you kill?

Now you can shoot at the targets without any fear of hurting civilians. If you see a line of Soldiers, kill the one who you think is the officer. Then, shoot the communications officer, then the MG [machine–gunner] – then the doctor – if he's there, you'll know by the red cross on his arm – (you don't need to respect the Geneva Treaty as long as the enemy does not respect it) and shoot at the Soldiers.

The first one is the Soldier (second from right) because he has a MG, heavy machine gun. Then is the stupid Soldier on the left. He is a very easy target (look how he is elevated from the ground), then the Soldier or the reporter carrying the camera. First, because the camera can be used as binoculars; second, it is the most difficult thing to hide the death of a reporter in Iraq.

PHOTO REDACTED

If you said the Soldiers, you are wrong. Kill the gunner on the left; then, the driver on the right.

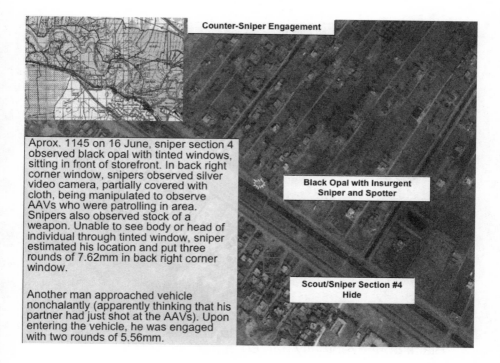

Counter-Sniper Engagement

Aprox. 1145 on 16 June, sniper section 4 observed black opal with tinted windows, sitting in front of storefront. In back right corner window, snipers observed silver video camera, partially covered with cloth, being manipulated to observe AAVs who were patrolling in area. Snipers also observed stock of a weapon. Unable to see body or head of individual through tinted window, sniper estimated his location and put three rounds of 7.62mm in back right corner window.

Another man approached vehicle nonchalantly (apparently thinking that his partner had just shot at the AAVs). Upon entering the vehicle, he was engaged with two rounds of 5.56mm.

Black Opal with Insurgent Sniper and Spotter

Scout/Sniper Section #4 Hide

U.S. forces have launched operations to counter the Iraqi insurgents' deadly snipers. In documenting one successful counter-sniper arrangement, U.S. forces also revealed how well equipped the terrorists' snipers are.

West field of view from sniper hide at initial occupation.
Black opal eventually parked in front of storefront.

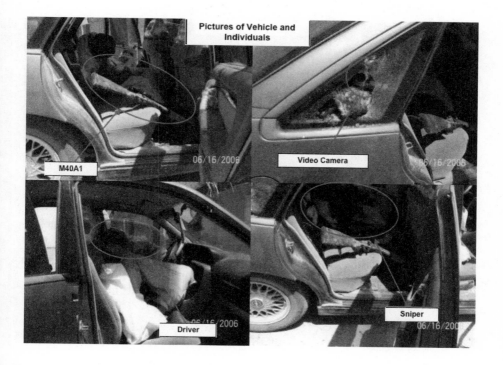

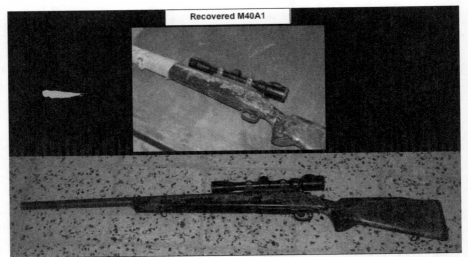

Recovered M40A1

Recovered M40A1 (SN: E6546973), confirmed as
belonging to 2/4 sniper team, who were killed in Ramadi
on 21 June 2004. Scope was Tasco 3x9, 32mm objective
lens, with illuminated reticle.

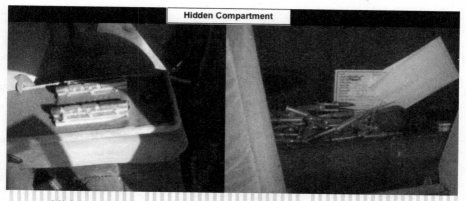

Hidden Compartment

Hidden compartment between trunk and rear seats of vehicle. Homemade locking lugs (picture on left), allowed compartment to be internally locked. Cursory search of the vehicle would not reveal compartment.

Contents of Hidden Compartment

Bushnell laser range finder, approximately (75) rounds of 7.62 (FN general purpose rounds), (1) FN Browning Hi-Power Pistol (SN: 45PZ33072), (1) 9mm pistol magazine, (1) M16 magazine, (1) grenade, a second digital video camera, (2) new video cassettes, assorted cassette tapes, and (2) complete sets of fake license plates.
Video camera contained five minutes of footage recording locally patrolling AAVs, specifically focused on hatch of vehicle commander.

ID Cards

Faris Mohamed Abid (driver/spotter)
DOB: 10 Aug 1965
POB: Ramadi
Wife: Zaroba Felah

Ihab Mohamed Abbas (sniper)
DOB: 1 Jan 1975
POB: Ramadi
Wife: Kareema Ismail

Front License Plate of Black Opal

Underneath Front License Plate

Rear License Plate

Underneath Rear License Plate

GPS CLASS FOR JIHADIST

THIS GPS CLASS TAUGHT USING THE GARMIN GPS-72, CONSISTING OF SEVEN VIDEOS, WAS POSTED ON A RADICAL WEBSITE BY AN UNIDENTIFIED SAUDI ARABIAN MALE, ON 3 AUG 05. THE CLASS APPEARS TO HAVE BEEN TAUGHT ON THE MORNING OF 26 JUN 05 (DATE/TIME ON THE GPS SCREEN). THE ACTUAL LOCATION WHERE THE CLASS WAS TAUGHT (VICINITY RIYADH, SAUDI ARABIA) CAN BE CLEARLY SEEN ON THE GPS SCREEN MAP. [ANALYST NOTE: AFTER VIEWING THE FIRST FEW CLIPS IN VIDEO #1, IT QUICKLY BECOMES APPARENT THAT THIS CLASS SEEMS TO BE DIRECTED AT FOREIGN JIHADISTS WHO MAY WANT TO NAVIGATE ACROSS THE BORDER INTO IRAQ. A MUJAHIDIN KNEELING NEXT TO HIS SWORD BEGINS VIDEO #1 WITH A CALL FOR MUJAHIDIN TO USE GPS TO WAGE JIHAD.]

(NOT TRANSLATED)

SOURCE: http://www.infovlad.net/; http://www.infovlad.net/?p=212

3

The U.S. Army produced this report revealing how foreign terrorists are infiltrating Iraq using handheld GPS devices. As the report shows, radical terrorist groups in Saudi Arabia offer classes to foreign fighters on how to navigate with GPS devices.

LOCATION OF GPS CLASS

CURRENT LOCATION

• NOTE THE CLASS LOCATION IS SHOWN ON THE GPS SCREEN:

    LAT: 23 DEG, 42 MIN, 689 SECONDS
    LONG: 047 DEG, 06 MIN, 532 SECONDS

• CLASS LOCATION IS VICINITY AL KHARJ, WHICH IS SOUTH OF RIYADH, SAUDI ARABIA

• RIYADH IS LOCATED AT LAT 24° 39' N, LONG 046° 42' E

SOURCES: http://crusader.rulez.jp/files/GPS72-2.wmv; http://crusader.rulez.jp/files/GPS72-3.wmv; http://www.bcca.org/misc/qiblih/latlong_oc.html#SAUDIxARABIA

4

DCSINT

FOREIGN JIHADISTS GUIDED BY GPS & "INSURGENTS' HOLY WAR MAP" ON INTERNET

ANALYST NOTE: PRIOR TO THE GPS CLASS BEING POSTED ON 3 AUG 05, A GROUP OF MESSAGES WERE POSTED ON THE INTERNET IN LATE JUN 05 (MESSAGE ENTITLED: "THE WAY TO THE COUNTRY OF THE TWO RIVERS") THAT PROVIDED GREAT DETAIL AND ADVICE TO FOREIGN FIGHTERS WANTING TO CROSS THE BORDER INTO IRAQ.

THE LEVEL OF DETAIL DISCUSSED IN THESE MESSAGES PROVIDES A CLEAR TERRAIN GUIDE FOR FOREIGN JIHADISTS, WANTING TO INFILTRATE IRAQ. THESE MESSAGES COULD PROVIDE SUPPORT TO THE ASSUMPTION THAT WAHHABI/JIHADIST GROUPS IN THE REGION MAY BE TURNING TO OFF-THE-SHELF GPS DEVICES TO GUIDE THEIR FIGHTERS INTO IRAQ, AS INDICATED BY THESE SEVEN VIDEOS ON THE GPS. A BRIEF DISCUSSION OF THESE MESSAGES FOLLOWS:

SOURCES: http://www.adnki.com/index_2Level.php?cat=Terrorism&loid=8.0.177662212&par=0 (ITALIAN NEWS SITE); http://www.infovlad.net/?p=212

6

DCSINT

"THE WAY TO THE COUNTRY OF THE TWO RIVERS"

BAGHDAD, 16 JUNE (AKI) - A MESSAGE ENTITLED "THE WAY TOWARDS THE COUNTRY OF THE TWO RIVERS," POSTED ON THE ISLAMIC "FIRDAWS" FORUM ON THE INTERNET ADVISES FOREIGN JIHADISTS TO CROSS INTO IRAQ FROM SYRIA.

THIS MESSAGE POSTED BY A 'DOCTOR ISLAM' (AL-MUHJHIR AL-ISLAMI), ASSERTS THAT THE SYRIAN-IRAQ BORDER IS THE MOST USED ENTRY POINT BY THE 'MUJAHIDIN.' DOCTOR ISLAM'S INITIAL MESSAGE AND FOLLOW-ON MESSAGES GIVE GREAT DETAIL EXPLAINING WHICH AREAS ALONG THE SYRIAN-IRAQ BORDER TO USE AS CROSSING POINTS AND WHICH AREAS TO AVOID, INCLUDING A TERRAIN DESCRIPTION, HOW TO BUILD RAPPORT WITH THE LOCAL POPULACE AND WHICH LOCAL SYRIAN LEADERS CANNOT BE TRUSTED.

A SELECTED EXCERPT FOLLOWS ON THE NEXT FEW SLIDES:

SOURCES: ARTICLE ENTITLED, "IRAQ: INSURGENTS' HOLY WAR MAP ON INTERNET" AT LINK
http://www.adnki.com/index_2Level.php?cat=Terrorism&loid=8.0.177662212&par=0; http://www.infovlad.net/?p=212

7

"THE WAY TO THE COUNTRY OF THE TWO RIVERS"

A SELECTED EXCERPT FROM DOCTOR ISLAM'S MESSAGES:

...THE SYRIAN-IRAQI BORDER RUNS FOR SOME 500 KILOMETERS:
ZONE A) ALONG THE FIRST 230 KILOMETERS IN THE NORTH WHERE THE
KURDS LIVE THE BORDER IS MARKED BY THE RIVER TIGRIS. THIS IS THE
TOUGHEST TRACT TO CROSS, WITH FRONTIER PATROLS DEPLOYED EVERY 10
KILOMETERS ALONG THE FIRST 130 KILOMETERS.
ZONE B) IS THE BEST AREA IN WHICH TO CROSS INTO IRAQ... FOR THE
FOLLOWING REASONS:
1) THE STRONG BONDS LINKING THE ARAB TRIBES ON BOTH SIDES OF THE BORDER.
2) THE SYMPATHY SHOWN BY THESE PEOPLE TOWARDS THE MUJAHIDIN FIGHTERS.
3) THE FERVENT ATTACHMENT OF THESE PEOPLE TOWARDS ISLAM AND ARAB TRADITIONS.
4) THE HATRED THEY HAVE FOR THE SYRIAN REGIME.
5) THE TIES BETWEEN THE LOCAL SHEIKS AND THOSE IN SAUDI ARABIA, IRAQ AND KUWAIT, IN
PARTICULAR WITH THOSE OF THE SHAMR, AL-BAKARA, AL-AKIDAT, AL-BUKHRIS TRIBES...
6) THE FEELING THAT THEY HAVE BEEN ABANDONED BY THE SYRIAN REGIME WHICH EXTRACTS 60
PERCENT OF ITS OIL, GRAIN, COTTON AND BARLEY EXPORTS FROM HERE, PROVIDING NOTHING IN
RETURN...

[ANALYST NOTE: ONLY GRAMMAR/MISSPELLINGS WERE CORRECTED]

"THE WAY TO THE COUNTRY OF THE TWO RIVERS"

EXCERPT CONTINUED:

7) OF THE 12.2 MILLION PEOPLE ORIGINATING FROM SYRIA'S DIR AL-ZUR REGION, SOME 350,000 WORK IN THE GULF STATES, SO IT IS EASY FOR YOU TO BEFRIEND THEM. THEY WILL TEACH YOU THE BEST WAY TO CROSS THEIR COUNTRY TO REACH IRAQ.
8) IT WILL TAKE YOU A HALF-HOUR WALK TO REACH THE IRAQI CITY OF QAIM (POPULATION 50,000) IF YOU SET OFF FROM THE DENSELY POPULATED CITY OF AL-BUKAMAL IN SYRIA...
9) THE HIGH LEVEL OF INTENSITY IN CLASHES WITH THE AMERICANS IS SOMETHING WHICH IS BEING MAINTAINED TO KEEP THEM OCCUPIED AND THUS EASE THE TASK FOR MUJAHIDIN CROSSING THE BORDER...
10) SOME OF THE VILLAGES ALONG THE BORDER ARE DIVIDED INTO SYRIAN AND IRAQI SECTORS.
11) PEOPLE IN THE REGION SPEAK AN IRAQI DIALECT VERY SIMILAR TO THE ONE SPOKEN IN THE GULF STATES.

[ANALYST NOTE: GRAMMAR/MISSPELLINGS WERE CORRECTED]

SOURCES: http://www.adnki.com/index_2Level.php?cat=Terrorism&loid=8.0.177662212&par=0; http://www.infovlad.net/?p=212

"THE WAY TO THE COUNTRY OF THE TWO RIVERS"

DOCTOR ISLAM FURTHER INSISTED THAT ALL WOULD-BE INSURGENTS AVOID ENTERING IRAQ FROM THE SOUTHERN "ZONE C" THAT RUNS ALONG THE PROVINCES OF HOMS IN SYRIA AND AL-ANBAR IN IRAQ. HE STATES THIS AREA IS HEAVILY PATROLLED BY SYRIAN MILITARY UNITS AND THAT DAMASCUS HAS SET UP "UNOFFICIAL PRISONS" IN THE AREA.

HE REPORTS THAT "MOST OF THOSE ARRESTED ON CHARGES OF TRYING TO CROSS THE BORDER HAVE BEEN HANDED OVER TO THE SYRIAN SECRET AGENTS BY THE MUFTI OF ALEPPO, AHMAD HASUN, KNOWN AS ONE OF THE DEADLIEST ENEMIES OF THE SALAFIST JIHADIST FACTION." DOCTOR ISLAM ALSO ADVISES, "DON'T CARRY A LOT OF CASH WITH YOU, THE AREA [ZONE B] IS ECONOMICAL AND YOU'LL ONLY NEED 300 US DOLLARS TO LODGE FOR 15 DAYS AT A FOUR STAR HOTEL. PETROL COSTS 10 DOLLARS FOR A JERRY-CAN."

SOURCES: http://www.adnki.com/index_2Level.php?cat=Terrorism&loid=8.0.177662212&par=0;
http://www.infovlad.net/?p=212

10

ABOUT THE GARMIN GPS-72

THE GPS 72 IS A LOW-COST SOLUTION FOR LAND OR MARINE NAVIGATION DESIGNED TO PROVIDE PRECISE GPS POSITIONING USING CORRECTION DATA OBTAINED FROM THE WIDE AREA AUGMENTATION SYSTEM (WAAS). THE GPS 72 CAN PROVIDE POSITION ACCURACY TO LESS THAN THREE METERS WHEN RECEIVING WAAS CORRECTIONS. THIS RUGGED, WATERPROOF, UNSINKABLE GPS RECEIVER OFFERS A LARGE, 4-LEVEL GRAYSCALE SCREEN. IT'S DESIGNED AS THE NEXT GENERATION IN BASIC, ENTRY-LEVEL GARMIN® GPS.

FEATURES INCLUDE:
- BACKLIT DISPLAY AND KEYPAD
- PERMANENT USER DATA STORAGE; NO MEMORY BATTERY REQUIRED
- 500 USER WAYPOINTS WITH NAME AND GRAPHIC SYMBOL; 50 REVERSIBLE ROUTES
- POSITION FORMATS INCLUDE LAT/LON, UTM, LORAN TDS, MAIDENHEAD, MGRS, AND USER GRID
- AUDIBLE ALARMS FOR ANCHOR DRAG, ARRIVAL, OFF-COURSE, PROXIMITY WAYPOINT, AND CLOCK
- TRIP COMPUTER PROVIDES ODOMETER, STOPPED TIME, MOVING AVERAGE, OVERALL AVERAGE, TOTAL TIME, MAX SPEED, AND MORE
- AUTOMATIC TRACK LOG; 10 SAVED TRACKS LET YOU RETRACE YOUR PATH IN BOTH DIRECTIONS
- BUILT-IN CELESTIAL TABLES FOR BEST TIME TO FISH, PLUS SUN AND MOON CALCULATIONS

11

ANALYST COMMENTS

- RADICAL/TERRORIST GROUPS IN SAUDI ARABIA ARE TEACHING FOREIGN FIGHTERS HOW TO NAVIGATE WITH GPS.
- JIHADISTS ARE FILMING THEIR GPS CLASSES AND ARE POSTING THEM ON THE WEB, TO INSTRUCT OTHER FOREIGN FIGHTERS ON HOW TO NAVIGATE WITH SUCH DEVICES.
- EXPERIENCED JIHADISTS ARE POSTING MESSAGES ON RADICAL WEBSITES, ADVISING OTHER FOREIGN FIGHTERS HOW TO BEST INFILTRATE IRAQ.
- THESE GPS DEVICES COULD BE USED FOR TARGETING, ONCE TRANSPORTED INTO IRAQ (NOTE: GARMIN CLAIMS THEIR SYSTEM IS ACCURATE WITHIN 3 METERS WITH WAAS CORRECTION DATA).
- THE GARMIN GPS SYSTEMS ARE PRODUCED IN THE KANSAS CITY, KANSAS METRO AREA.

POCs: Mr. Vincent McLean, vincent.mclean@leavenworth.army.mil or Ms. Penny Mellies, penny.mellies@leavenworth.army.mil at 913-684-7920/22; DSN: 552-7920, 700 Scott Ave, Bldg 53, ADCSINT, TRADOC, Ft Leavenworth, KS 66027

12

A Line in the Sand:
Confronting the Threat at the Southwest Border

PREPARED BY THE MAJORITY STAFF OF THE
HOUSE COMMITTEE ON HOMELAND SECURITY
SUBCOMMITTEE ON INVESTIGATIONS
MICHAEL T. McCAUL, Chairman

If we are serious about protecting our country, we need to know who's coming into our country. In these excerpts from a congressional report, we see how dangerous criminals and, yes, terrorists are coming into the United States over the Mexican border.

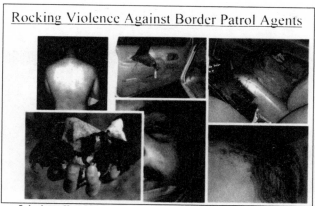

Injuries suffered by Border Patrol agents from rocks thrown

According to Texas Homeland Security Director Steve McCraw, the ruthlessness and violence of these criminal networks are unprecedented. At one time, members or associates of Mexican drug cartels would drop the drugs or abandon their vehicles when confronted by U.S. law enforcement. Similarly, human smugglers would simply give up when approached or stopped on the highway. This is no longer the case. The drug cartels no longer tolerate compliance. Loads of both drugs and humans are vigorously protected by direct confrontation, high speed chases, and standoffs at the Rio Grande River.[64]

In today's climate, U.S. Border Patrol agents are fired upon from across the river and troopers and sheriff's deputies are subject to attacks with automatic weapons while the cartels retrieve their contraband. In May 2006, the Zapata County Sheriff's Office received information that the cartels immediately across the border plan to threaten or kill as many police officers as possible on the United States' side.[65]

---

[64] *Criminal Activity and Violence Along the Southern Border: Hearing Before the Subcomm. on Investigations of the House Comm. on Homeland Security*, 109th Cong., (Aug. 16, 2006) at 2 (written Statement of Steve McCraw, Director, Governor's Office of Homeland Security, Tex).
[65] Interview by Subcomm. Staff with Sigifredo Gonzalez in Laredo, Tex (Aug. 23, 2006).

Laredo, Texas Incident 12/28/2005

On December 28, 2005, while apprehending a group of undocumented aliens, two border patrol agents were fired upon by an unknown assailant on the Mexican side of the border. A CBP Remote Video Surveillance camera operator was able to capture pictures of the likely assailants, shown above. Since this incident, the same assailant (2nd from the left) has been tied to three other incidents involving shots fired at CBP Border Patrol Agents.

Between May 2004 and July 2006 there have been forty-nine reported abductions of U.S. citizens in the region between the Texas cities of Del Rio and Brownsville. Thirty-four of these abductions occurred in Nuevo Laredo and involved U.S. citizens who had crossed the border. Twenty-three victims were released by their captors, nine victims remain missing, and two are confirmed dead. These numbers likely represent only a fraction of the actual occurrences, as many kidnappings of U.S. citizens go unreported.[66]

Yvette Martinez, 27, and her friend Brenda Cisneros, 23, are among nine Americans who the FBI says have simply disappeared along the border in the last two years. Martinez and Cisneros crossed the border in September 2004 to attend a concert in Nuevo Laredo – and never came back. The FBI revealed in testimony that alleged members of Los Zetas are believed to have kidnapped Martinez and Cisneros.[67] The violent brazenness of these criminal groups knows no limits. In broad daylight, a young man was gunned down in a Laredo parking lot as his pregnant wife looked on. The ambush had all the markings of a cartel assassination.[68] Webb County, Texas Sheriff Rick Flores is concerned with the level of brutality that accompanies the cartels as they move their merchandise across the border. Flores says these cartels show no mercy for women or children.[69]

---

[66] *Combating Violence at the U.S. Southwest Border: Hearing Before the Subcomm. on Crime, Terrorism, and Homeland Security and the Subcomm. on Immigration, Border Security and Claims of the House Comm. on Judiciary,* 109th Cong. (Nov. 2005) at 1-2 (written Statement of Chris Swecker, Assistant Director, Criminal Investigative Division, Federal Bureau of Investigation).
[67] *Id.*
[68] Aug. 23 Interview with Flores.
[69] *Id.*

II.   Illegal Alien Crimes Against U.S. Citizens

Not all illegal aliens are crossing into the United States to find work. Law enforcement officials indicate that there are individuals coming across the border who are forced to leave their home countries because of their criminal activity. These dangerous criminals are fleeing the law in other countries and seeking refuge in the United States. For instance, it is known that many of the operatives of cartels in Mexico actually live in the United States. Information received by several law enforcement agencies indicates these criminals are living in our communities and that they come to the U.S. to escape the possibility of apprehension in Mexico.[90]

The Violent Crimes Institute conducted a 12 month in-depth study of illegal immigrants who committed sex crimes and murders for the time period of January 1999 through April 2006. This study makes it clear that the U.S. faces a dangerous threat from sexual predators that cross the U.S. borders illegally. [91]

The Institute analyzed 1,500 cases in depth, including serial rapes, serial murders, sexual homicides, and child molestation committed by illegal immigrants. Police reports, public records, interviews with police, and media accounts were all included. Offenders were located in thirty-six states, with the most of the offenders were located in States with the highest numbers of illegal immigrants. California was ranked first, followed by Texas, Arizona, New Jersey, New York, and Florida. [92]

Based on an estimated illegal immigrant population of 12,000,000 and the fact that young males make up more of this population than the general U.S. population, the Institute concluded that sex offenders in the illegal immigrant group make up a higher percentage. ICE reports and public records show sex offenders comprising 2% of illegals apprehended. Based on this 2% figure, which is conservative, the Institute estimates that there are approximately 240,000 illegal immigrant sex offenders in the United States. [93]

The study concluded, when applied to ongoing illegal immigration at the borders, these estimates translate to 93 sex offenders and twelve serial sexual offenders coming across U.S. borders illegally per day. The 1,500 offenders in this study had a total of 5,999 victims. Each sex offender averaged four victims. This puts the estimate for victimization numbers around 960,000 for the 88 months examined in this study.[94]

The violence of illegal aliens is not confined to border communities. Residents and law enforcement in the interior cities are also vulnerable to criminals crossing the border. The following are examples of crimes committed by illegal aliens:

---

[90] *Id.*

[91] Deborah Schurman-Kauflin, PhD., *The Dark Side of Illegal Immigration: Nearly One Million Sex Crimes Committee by Illegal Immigrants in the United States*, The Violent Crimes Institute, (2006).

[92] *Id.*

[93] *Id.*

[94] *Id.*

- In testimony before the House Committee on Homeland Security's Subcommittee on Investigations, Carrie Ruiz, a Houston resident, described how her 17 year old daughter was murdered in October 1999 by an illegal immigrant from Venezuela who escaped prosecution by returning to his home country. Ruiz's daughter was stabbed more than thirty-nine times after she helped authorities identify a gang member.

- On February 10, 2005, a high-ranking member of the Mara Salvatrucha (MS-13), was apprehended in Brooks County, Texas. He had been previously deported at least four times. This MS-13 gang member is believed to have been responsible for the killing of twenty-eight persons, including six children, and the wounding of fourteen others, in a bus explosion in his native country. Information was received in late April of this year that he was on his way back into the United States, or that he was already in the country, and was threatening to assassinate any officer that attempted to apprehend him. [95]

- On March 22, 2006, Texas State Trooper Steven Stone was shot six times at point blank range by two illegal aliens during a routine traffic stop. Ramon Ramos and Francisco Saucedo were charged with fourteen counts of aggravated assault on a public servant. An investigation showed that Ramos had been criminally deported from the United States on two different occasions on Federal weapons and drug charges. Ramos had been living illegally in the United States for approximately three to four years prior to the March 22 shooting.

  On the night of the shooting, Ramos and Saucedo were in possession of body armor, a rifle modified for automatic fire, a handgun modified for automatic fire, two or more handguns, numerous knives, drugs and alcohol. [96]

- On June 27, 2006, a teenage girl from Mexia, Texas was forced off the road by two illegal aliens and kidnapped. She was sexually assaulted by both men. The two illegals tried unsuccessfully to break her neck and strangle her. They then dragged her out of the car and put her into a ditch where they began kicking, beating, and stabbing her with broken glass. She sustained massive injuries to her head, face and upper body. After the suspects left her for dead, she was able to walk about one-half mile to the nearest house and ask for help. The suspects are identified as Noel Darwin Hernandez and Javier Guzman Martinez. An immigration hold has been placed on each suspect. [97]

---

[95] *Border Vulnerabilities and InterNational Terrorism Part II: Hearing Before the Subcomm. On InterNational Terrorism and Nonproliferation of the House Comm. On International Relations*, 109th Cong. (July 7, 2006) at 3 (written Statement of Sigifredo Gonzalez, Sheriff, Zapata County, Tex.).
[96] *Criminal Activity and Violence Along the Southern Border: Hearing Before the Subcomm. on Investigations of the House Comm. on Homeland Security*, 109th Cong., (Aug. 16, 2006) (statement of Steven Stone, State Trooper, Tex.).
[97] Mike Anderson, *Texas Woman Spent Two Hours 'in Hell' After Being Beaten, Raped*, WACO TRIBUNE-HERALD, June 30, 2006.

- On September 21, 2006, in Houston, Texas an illegal immigrant from Mexico, Juan Leonardo Quintero, was charged in with capital murder in the shooting death of Houston Police Officer Rodney Johnson. Quintero had been deported in the past. His record shows in 1998 he was charged with indecency with a child.[98]

On September 29, 2006, one week after Officer Johnson was killed by an illegal alien, Houston Mayor Bill White announced a change in the way Houston Police officers process suspected illegal immigrants. The Houston police will fingerprint suspected illegal immigrants detained on minor violations, and those with identification police believe to be fraudulent. That information will then be provided to Federal authorities.[99]

III.   Vulnerability to Terrorist Infiltration

The number of aliens other than Mexican ("OTMs") illegally crossing the border has grown at an alarming rate over the past several years. Based on U.S. Border Patrol statistics there were 30,147 OTMs apprehended in FY2003, 44,614 in FY2004, 165,178 in FY2005, and 108,025 in FY2006. Most of them were apprehended along the U.S. Southwest border.[100]

The sheer increase of OTMs coming across the border makes it more difficult for Border Patrol agents to readily identify and process each, thereby increasing the chances that a potential terrorist could slip through the system. Moreover, there is no concrete mechanism for determining how many OTMs evade apprehensions and successfully enter the country illegally.

The U.S. Department of Homeland Security (DHS) pays particular attention to OTMs apprehended by the Border Patrol who originate from thirty-five nations designated as "special interest" countries. According to Border Patrol Chief David Aguilar, special interest countries have been "designated by our intelligence community as countries that could export individuals that could bring harm to our country in the way of terrorism."[101]

Though the majority of overall apprehensions made by the Border Patrol occur in the Tucson sector of Arizona, the Texas border – specifically the McAllen sector – far outpaces the rest of the country in OTM and Special Interest Alien apprehensions. Since September 11, 2001, DHS has reported a 41% increase in arrests along the Texas/Mexico border of Special Interest Aliens.

---

[98] Jennifer Leahy, James Nielsen and Mike Tolson, *Illegal Immigrant Charged in HPD Shooting Death*, HOUSTON CHRONICLE, Sept. 22, 2006.

[99] Houston, Texas 11 News reports, Sept. 29, 2006 (3:18 PM).

[100] Information provided by U.S. Border Patrol to Subcomm. Staff. (Oct. 3, 2006).

[101] *Strengthening Border Security Between Ports of Entry: The Use of Technology to Protect Our Borders: Hearing Before the Subcomm. On Immigration, Border Security and Citizenship and the Subcomm. On Terrorism, Technology and Homeland Security of the Senate Comm. On the Judiciary*, 109th Cong. (Apr. 28, 2005) (written statement of David Aguilar, Chief, Border Patrol, U.S. Department of Homeland Security).

From FY2001 to March 2005, 88 percent of Special Interest Alien apprehensions for both the Southwest and Northern borders occurred in Texas. During that same period, 75 percent of Special Interest Alien apprehensions on the Southwest border occurred in the Laredo, McAllen, and Del Rio Sectors. Since September 11, 2001 to the present hundreds of illegal aliens from special interest countries (such as Iran, Jordan, Lebanon, Syria, Egypt, Saudi Arabia, Kuwait, Pakistan, Cuba, Brazil, Ecuador, China, Russia, Yemen, Albania, Yugoslavia and Afghanistan) were apprehended within the South Texas region alone.[102]

The data indicates that each year hundreds of illegal aliens from countries known to harbor terrorists or promote terrorism are routinely encountered and apprehended attempting to enter the U.S. illegally between Ports of Entry. Just recently, U.S. intelligence officials report that seven Iraqis were found in Brownsville, Texas in June 2006.[103] In August 2006, an Afghani man was found swimming across the Rio Grande River in Hidalgo, Texas;[104] as recently as October 2006, seven Chinese were apprehended in the Rio Grande Valley area of Texas.[105]

Items have been found by law enforcement officials along the banks of the Rio Grande River and inland that indicate possible ties to a terrorist organization or member of military units of Mexico.[106] A jacket with patches from countries where al Qa'ida is known to operate was found in Jim Hogg County, Texas by the Border Patrol. The patches on the jacket show an Arabic military badge with one depicting an airplane flying over a building and heading towards a tower, and another showing an image of a lion's head with wings and a parachute emanating from the animal. The bottom of one patch read "martyr," "way to eternal life" or "way to immortality."[107]

[102] Telephone Interview by Subcomm. Staff with Federal law enforcement personnel, in Wash. D.C. (Oct. 13, 2006).
[103] Interview by Subcomm. Staff with Federal law enforcement personnel, in McAllen, Tex. (Aug. 21, 2006).
[104] *Id.*
[105] Telephone Interview by Subcomm. Staff with Federal law enforcement personnel, in Wash. D.C. (Oct. 13, 2006).
[106] *Border Vulnerabilities and International Terrorism Part II: Hearing Before the Subcomm. On International Terrorism and Nonproliferation of the House Comm. On International Relations*, 109th Cong. (July 7, 2006) at 4 (written Statement of Sigifredo Gonzalez, Sheriff, Zapata County, Tex.).
[107] *Id.*

Military patches found along the Texas border.

On January 28, 2006, Border Patrol Chief David Aguilar was asked by a reporter from KGNS television station in Laredo, Texas, about the outcome of the investigation of the jacket. Chief Aguilar responded that the patches were not from al Qa'ida but from countries in which al Qa'ida was known to operate.[108]

According to ICE testimony, on September 8, 2004, ICE agents arrested Neeran Zaia and Basima Sesi. The human smuggling organization headed by Zaia specialized in smuggling Iraqi, Jordanian, and Syrian Nationals and was responsible for the movement of more than 200 aliens throughout the investigation.[109] The investigation was initiated when a confidential informant familiar with the organization reported ongoing smuggling activities by Zaia, who had been previously convicted of alien smuggling. Investigative efforts revealed that the aliens were smuggled from the Middle East to staging areas in Central and South America. Once in these staging areas, the conspirators would arrange to smuggle the aliens from these sites into the U.S. or its territories.[110]

Members of Hezbollah, the Lebanon-based terrorist organization, have already entered to the United States across our Southwest border. On March 1, 2005, Mahmoud Youssef Kourani pleaded guilty to providing material support to Hezbollah.[111] Kourani is an

---

[108] *Federal Strategies to End Border Violence: Hearing Before the Subcomm. On Immigration, Border Security and Citizenship and the Subcomm. On Terrorism, Technology, and Homeland Security of the Senate Comm. On the Judiciary*, 109th Cong. (Mar. 1, 2006) at 4 (written Statement of A. D'Wayne Jernigan, Sheriff, Val Verde County, Tex.).

[109] *Setting Post 9/11 Priorities at the Bureau of Immigration and Customs Enforcement: Hearing Before the Subcomm. on National Security, Emerging Threats and International Relations of the House Comm. On Government Reform*, 109th Cong. (Mar. 28, 2006) at 4 (written Statement of Robert A. Schoch, Deputy Assistant Director, National Security Division, Office of Investigations).

[110] *Id.*

[111] Press Release, U.S. Attorney, Eastern District of Michigan, Department of Justice, Mar. 1, 2005; *available at* http://detroit.fbi.gov/dojpressrel/pressrel05/hizballahsupport030105.

illegal alien who had been smuggled across the U.S.-Mexico border after bribing a Mexican consular official in Beirut for a visa to travel to Mexico. Kourani and a Middle Eastern traveling partner then paid coyotes in Mexico to guide them into the United States. Kourani established residence among the Lebanese expatriate community in Dearborn, Michigan and began soliciting funds for Hezbollah terrorists back home in Lebanon. He is the brother of the Hezbollah chief of military operations in southern Lebanon.

In December 2002, Salim Boughader Mucharrafille, a café owner in Tijuana, Mexico, was arrested for illegally smuggling more than two hundred Lebanese illegally into the United States, including several believed to have terrorist ties to Hezbollah.[112] Just last month Robert L. Boatwright, Assistant Chief Patrol Agent of the El Paso Texas Sector, reported, "We have apprehended people from countries that support terrorism...they were thoroughly debriefed and there was a tremendous amount of information collected from them."[113]

Statements made by high-ranking Mexican officials prior to and following the September 11, 2001 terrorist attacks indicate that one or more Islamic terrorist organizations has sought to establish a presence in Mexico. In May 2001, former Mexican National security adviser and ambassador to the United Nations, Adolfo Aguilar Zinser, reported, that "Spanish and Islamic terrorist groups are using Mexico as a refuge."[114]

Federal Bureau of Investigation Director Robert Mueller has confirmed in testimony "that there are individuals from countries with known al-Qa'ida connections who are changing their Islamic surnames to Hispanic-sounding names and obtaining false Hispanic identities, learning to speak Spanish and pretending to be Hispanic immigrants.[115]

These examples highlight the dangerous intersection between traditional transnational criminal activities, such as human and drug smuggling, and more ominous threats to national security. Sheriff Sigifredo Gonzalez summed it up this way: "I dare to say that at any given time, daytime or nighttime, one can get on a boat and traverse back and forth between Texas and Mexico and not get caught. If smugglers can bring in tons of marijuana and cocaine at one time and can smuggle 20 to 30 persons at one time, one can just imagine how easy it would be to bring in 2 to 3 terrorists or their weapons of mass destruction across the river and not be detected. Chances of apprehension are very slim."[116]

---

[112] Associated Press, *Terror-Linked Migrants Channeled into U.S.*, FOXNEWS.COM, July 3, 2005; *available at* http://www.foxnews.com/story/0,2933,161473,00.html.
[113] Chris Roberts, *Agency Focuses Fight Against Smuggling, Terrorism*, EL PASO TIMES, Sept. 13, 2006.
[114] Ramon J. Miro, *Organized Crime and Terrorist Activity in Mexico, 1999-2002*, Library of Congress, (Feb. 2003) at 43.
[115] *FBI FY 2006 Budget Request: Hearing Before the House Comm. On Appropriations*, 108th Cong. (Mar.8, 2005) (Written Statement of Robert Mueller, Director, Federal Bureau of Investigations).
[116] *Border Vulnerabilities and International Terrorism Part II: Hearing Before the Subcomm. On International Terrorism and Nonproliferation of the House Comm. On International Relations*, 109th Cong. (July 7, 2006) at 2 (written Statement of Sigifredo Gonzalez, Sheriff, Zapata County, Tex.).

Furthermore, according to senior U.S. military and intelligence officials, Venezuela is emerging as a potential hub of terrorism in the Western Hemisphere, providing assistance to Islamic radicals from the Middle East and other terrorists.[117]

General James Hill, commander of U.S. Southern Command, has warned the United States faces a growing risk from both Middle Eastern terrorists relocating to Latin America and terror groups originating in the region. General Hill said groups such as Hezbollah had established bases in Latin America. These groups are taking advantage of smuggling hotspots, such as the tri-border area of Brazil, Argentina and Paraguay, and Venezuela's Margarita Island, to channel funds to terrorist groups around the world.[118]

Venezuela is providing support—including identity documents—that could prove useful to radical Islamic groups, say some U.S. officials. The Venezuelan government has issued thousands of cedulas, the equivalent of Social Security cards, to people from places such as Cuba, Columbia, and Middle Eastern nations that host foreign terrorist organizations. The U.S. officials believe that the Venezuelan government is issuing the documents to people who should not be getting them and that some of these cedulas could be subsequently used to obtain Venezuelan passports and even American visas, which could allow the holder to elude immigration checks and enter the United States.[119] Recently, several Pakistanis were apprehended at the U.S.-Mexican border with fraudulent Venezuelan documents.[120]

"Hugo Chavez, President of Venezuela, has been clearly talking to Iran about uranium," said a senior administration official quoted by the Washington Times. Chavez has made several trips to Iran and voiced solidarity with the country's hard-line mullahs. He has hosted Iranian officials in Caracas, endorsed Tehran's nuclear ambitions and expressed support for the insurgency in Iraq. The Times reports Venezuela is also talking with Hamas about sending representatives to Venezuela to raise money for the militant group's newly elected Palestinian government as Chavez seeks to build an anti-U.S. axis that also includes Fidel Castro's Cuba. "I am on the offensive," Chavez said on the al Jazeera television network, "because attack is the best form of defense. We are waging an offensive battle...."[121]

Given all that is happening in Chavez's Venezuela, some American officials regret that terrorism is seen chiefly as a Middle East problem and that the United States needs to look looking to protect its southern flank. A U.S. intelligence official expressed concern that "Counterterrorism issues are not being aggressively pursued in this hemisphere." Another intelligence official stated terror suspects held at Guantanamo Bay are not being interrogated about connections to Latin America. The bottom line, when it comes to

---

[117] Linda Robinson, U.S. News & World Report, "Terror Close to Home," October 6, 2003.
[118] Andy Webb-Vidal, *Terror Groups 'Relocating to U.S.'s Backyard,'* THE FINANCIAL TIMES, March 5, 2003.
[119] *Id.*
[120] Interview by Subcomm. Staff with Federal investigator (Sept. 18, 2006).
[121] Rowan Scarborough, *Chavez Turns to Iran on Military, Uranium,* WASHINGTON TIMES, Apr. 10, 2006.

terrorism so close to U.S. shores, says the official, "We don't even know what we don't know."[122]

Islamic radical groups that support Hamas, Hezbollah and Islamiya Al Gamat are all active in Latin America. These groups generate funds through money laundering, drug trafficking, and arms deals, making millions of dollars every year via their multiple illicit activities. These cells reach back to the Middle East and extend to this hemisphere the sophisticated global support structure of international terrorism. While threats to our nation from international terrorism are well known, lesser known threats spawned by narcoterrorism reach deeply into this country.[123]

Federal law enforcement entities estimate they apprehend approximately 10 to 30 percent of illegal aliens crossing the border.[124] U.S. intelligence officials along the southwest border, on the other hand, are less optimistic. To be sure, it is unclear how many illegal aliens of any nationality evade capture by law enforcement each year and succeed in entering the United States illegally. It is especially difficult to provide the total number of Special Interest Aliens entering the U.S. illegally because they pay larger amounts of money ($15,000 to $60,000 per alien) to employ the more effective Mexican alien smuggling organizations and are less likely to be apprehended.

One thing, however, is known for certain – hundreds of people from countries known to harbor terrorists or promote terrorism are caught trying to enter the United States illegally along the land border, and the massive flow of immigrants and our porous border create various and abundant opportunities for concealment. Given the ever-present threat posed by al-Qa'ida and other terrorist organizations – a threat that has been underscored by the recent events in London and the vulnerability of our borders – the need for immediate action to enforce our borders could not be more apparent.

IV.   Texas Border Security Initiatives

In response to the increasing criminal activity and violence along the Southwest border, on February 9, 2006, the State of Texas, in partnership with the Federal government, launched Operation Rio Grande. The strategy focuses on four key areas: 1) increased patrols and law enforcement presence; 2) centralized of command, control, and intelligence operations; 3) increased State funding and deployment of State resources for border security; and 4) enhanced utilization of technology to fight border crime.[125] By concentrating on these areas, Texas has mounted an aggressive defense to significantly reduce crime in areas of operations. When executed, these operations have significantly

---

[122] Linda Robinson, *Terror Close to Home*, U.S. NEWS AND WORLD REPORT, Oct. 6, 2003.

[123] Lt. Gen. James E. Hill, Commander, U.S. Southern Command, Remarks to the Association of the U.S. Army Annual Meeting, Wash., D.C., (Oct. 6, 2003).

[124]Interview by Subcomm. Staff with Federal law enforcement personnel, in McAllen, Tex. (Aug. 21, 2006).

[125] Information provided by Tex. Homeland Security Director Steve McCraw to Subcomm. Staff (Oct. 2006).

authority the Coast Guard currently possesses for vessels. The Act enhances border security through a "virtual fence" that deploys cameras, ground sensors, unmanned aerial vehicles and integrated surveillance technology, and an evaluation of the Northern border and determining what actions are needed to secure those areas.[146]

VI.   Conclusion

The Federal government has taken positive steps to secure its borders, but much more is needed to combat an increasingly powerful, sophisticated, and violent criminal network which has been successful in smuggling illegal contraband, human or otherwise, into our country. The growth of these criminal groups, along the Southwest border, and the potential for terrorists to exploit the vulnerabilities which they create, represents a real threat to America's national security.

It is imperative that immediate action be taken to enhance security along our nation's Southwest border. Greater control of the border can be achieved by:

- enhancing Border Patrol resources, including expanding agent training capacity, and technical surveillance abilities;
- constructing physical barriers in vulnerable and high-threat areas;
- implementing state-of-the-art technology, cameras, sensors, radar, satellite, and Unmanned Aerial Vehicles to ensure maximum coverage of the Nation's Southwest border;
- making permanent the "catch and return" policy;
- expanding the use of the expedited removal policy;
- establishing additional detention bed space;
- improving partnerships and information sharing among Federal, State, and local law enforcement;
- building a secure interoperable communications network for Border Patrol and state and local law enforcement;
- mandating a comprehensive risk assessment of all Southwest border Ports of Entry and international land borders to prevent the entry of terrorist and weapons of mass destruction;
- promoting both international and domestic policies that will deter further illegal entry into the United States; and
- Enhancing intelligence capabilities and information sharing with our Mexican counterparts and improving cooperation with the Mexican government to eradicate the Cartels.

The Subcommittee will continue its investigation of border security matters and plans to issue a more comprehensive report on the entire Southwest border. The Subcommittee will hold future hearings, as warranted, on border security.

---

[146] Press Release, House Committee on Homeland Security, *Four Major King-led Homeland Security Measures to Become Law*, Sept. 20, 2006.

NOTES

CHAPTER 1: RIGHT IN FRONT OF US

1. Tim Pritchard, "When Iraq Went Wrong," *New York Times,* December 5, 2006.

2. Brian Ross and Christopher Isham, "Three Foiled Hijack Plots Revealed in U.S. Document," ABCNews.com, June 21, 2006.

3. "Report: Hundreds of WMDs Found in Iraq," FoxNews.com, June 22, 2006.

CHAPTER 2: GETTING THE WAR ON TERROR RIGHT

1. Gary Berntsen, *Jawbreaker: The Attack on Bin Laden and al Qaeda: A Personal Account by the CIA's Key Field Commander* (New York: Crown, 2005).

2. Ibid.

3. Massoud Ansari, "Kandahar Dispatch: Return of Jihadi," New Republic Online, October 27, 2003, available at http://www.tnr.com/doc.mhtml?i=20031027&s=ansari102703.

4. "U.S. General: Training Afghan Army Will Take Years," *USA Today,* July 13, 2006.

5. "Afghanistan Security: Efforts to Establish Army and Police Have Made Progress, but Future Plans Need to Be Better Defined," U.S. Government Accountability Office, June 2005.

6. "Afghanistan Opium Survey 2006: Executive Summary," United Nations Office on Drugs and Crime, September 2006, available at http://www.unodc.org/pdf/execsummaryafg.pdf; Karen DeYoung, "Afghanistan Opium Crop Sets Record," *Washington Post,* December 2, 2006.

7. "State Sponsors: North Korea," Council on Foreign Relations, December 2005, available at http://www.cfr.org/publication/9364/.

8. Ibid.

9. "North Korea Demands Reactor First," CNN.com, September 19, 2005, available at http://www.cnn.com/2005/WORLD/asiapcf/09/19/korea.north.talks/index.html.

10. "Iran Bought Missiles from North Korea: Press," Agence France-Presse, December 16, 2005, available at http://www.defensenews.com/story.php?F=1415703&C=mideast.

11. Nazila Fathi, "Wipe Israel 'Off the Map,' Iranian Says," *International Herald Tribune,* October 27, 2005.

12. "Iran Bought Missiles from North Korea: Press," Agence France-Presse.

13. "The Iranian Threat: Bio: Mahmoud Ahmadinejad," *Jerusalem Post,* May 22, 2006.

14. "Iran Responsible for 1983 Marine Barracks Bombing, Judge Rules," CNN.com, May 30, 2003.

15. Peter Brookes, "Spooks, Lies & Videotape," The Heritage Foundation, July 6, 2004.

16. Dafna Linzer, "Iran Is Judged 10 Years from Nuclear Bomb: U.S. Intelligence Review Contrasts with Administration Statements," *Washington Post,* August 2, 2005.

17. Amir Taheri, "Tehran Terrorfest," *New York Post,* January 26, 2004.

18. "Hizballah/Hizbollah/Hizbullah/Hezbollah, Party of God, Islamic Jihad, Islamic Jihad for the Liberation of Palestine, Organization of the Oppressed on Earth, Revolutionary Justice Organization," Global Security, July 16, 2006.

19. "A Strategic Assessment of the Hizballah War: Defeating the Iranian-Syrian Axis in Lebanon," Jerusalem Center for Public Affairs, Institute for Contemporary Affairs, July 19, 2006.

20. "Threats to Canada's National Security," Canadian Security Intelligence Service, October 10, 2003, quoted in "Canada Admits: We're Terror

Haven," WorldNetDaily.com, March 2, 2004, available at http://worldnet daily.com/news/article.asp?ARTICLE_ID=37376.

21. Ibid.

22. "Bush Seeks Additional $600 Million for Tsunami Relief," Department of State, February 9, 2005.

23. "2006 Poll: Humanitarian Relief Sustains Change in Muslim Public Opinion," Terror Free Tomorrow, available at http://www.terrorfreetomorrow.org./articlenav.php?id=82.

24. Defense: FY2007 Authorization and Appropriations, updated May 31, 2006, Stephen Daggett, Specialist in National Defense Foreign Affairs, Defense, and Trade Division; Jim Lobe, "Special Forces, Big-Ticket Weapons Dominate Defense Plan," Inter Press Service, February 8, 2006.

25. Thom Shanker, "In Bill's Fine Print, Millions to Celebrate Victory," *New York Times*, October 4, 2006.

26. See http://www.thereligionofpeace.com/index.html#Attacks.

CHAPTER 3: THE PLAIN TRUTH ABOUT IRAQ

1. John Kerry's Statement on Iraq Before the War, U.S. Senate, October 9, 2002.

2. Sally B. Donnelly, "Getting the Lowdown on Iraq," *Time*, November 21, 2005, available at http://www.time.com/time/magazine/article/0,9171,113 2819,00.html.

3. "Rice: Thousands of Errors in Iraq," CNN.com, April 1, 2006.

4. Details of this time line derived from L. Paul Bremer III with Malcolm McConnell, *My Year in Iraq: The Struggle to Build a Future of Hope* (New York: Simon & Schuster, 2006), and from Nimrod Raphael: "Understanding Muqtada al-Sadr." *Middle East Quarterly*, Volume XI, Number 4, Fall 2004.

5. Bremer, *My Year in Iraq*, 121–22.

6. Ibid., 129–30.

7. Ibid., 131.

8. Ibid., 135.

9. Ibid., 147.

10. Ibid., 148.

11. Ibid., 166.

12. Ibid., 166.
13. Ibid., 190.
14. Ibid., 195.
15. Ibid., 197.
16. Ibid., 199.
17. Ibid., 199.
18. Ibid., 296.
19. Ibid., 312.
20. Ibid., 312.
21. Ibid., 312.
22. Ibid., 312.
23. Ibid., 313.
24. Ibid., 313.
25. Ibid., 326.
26. Ibid., 332.
27. Ellen Knickmeyer and Muhanned Saif Aldin, "Dozens of Iraqis Killed in Reprisals," *Washington Post,* October 16, 2006.
28. Edward Wong and Nazila Fathi, "Iraqi Leader Asks Iran for Help With Security," *New York Times,* September 12, 2006.
29. Scott Harris, "BTL: Special Forces Veteran Asserts the Iraq War Has Already Been Lost," Between the Lines, May 20, 2006.
30. Iraq Coalition Casualty Count, available at http://www.icasualties.org/oif/.

CHAPTER 4: THE THREATS WE FACE

1. "Investigators Tracing Terror Plot Money Trail," Associated Press, August 11, 2006.
2. "Experts Warn of Substantial Risk of WMD Attack: New Survey Predicts 70 Percent Chance of Attack in Next Decade," Reuters, June 22, 2005, available at http://www.msnbc.msn.com/id/8312212/.
3. Ibid.
4. Frank von Hippel, "Working in the White House on Nuclear Nonproliferation and Arms Control: A Personal Report," *Journal of the Federation of American Scientists,* Volume 48, No. 2, March/April 1995.
5. Nuclear Regulatory Commission, "Preliminary Observations on Efforts to Improve Security at Nuclear Power Plants," September 14, 2004, 6.

6. Author's interview with Robert Domenici.

7. Author's interview with Kevin Lynch.

8. John B. Stephenson, director, natural resources and environment, U.S. Government Accountability Office, Testimony Before the Subcommittee on Environment and Hazardous Materials, Committee on Energy and Commerce, House of Representatives, September 30, 2004.

9. "National Planning Scenarios," Homeland Security Council, April 2005.

10. Robert Lemos, "Cyberterrorism: The Real Risks," CNET News.com, August 27, 2002.

11. Brady McCombs, "Guard's Hands-off Approach Tightens Border Security," *Arizona Daily Star,* October 21, 2006.

12. "Army Tops Recruit Goal by Lowering Standards," Associated Press, October 9, 2006.

CHAPTER 5: THESE GUYS ARE SERIOUS

1. See "Improvised Explosive Devices (IEDs)—Iraq," GlobalSecurity.org, available at http://www.globalsecurity.org/military/intro/ied-iraq.htm.

2. For a detailed discussion, see "Improvised Explosive Devices (IEDs)/ Booby Traps," GlobalSecurity.org, available at http://www.globalsecurity. org/military/intro/ied.htm.

3. Jeffrey A. Slotnick, "Explosive Forces of Improvised Explosive Devices," SecurityDriver.com, available at http://securitydriver.com/aic/stories/ article-114.html.

4. Iraqi Casualty Count, available at http://icasualties.org/oif/IED.aspx.

5. For a more detailed discussion of Army sniper training, see Rod Powers, "Army Sniper School," About.com, available at http://usmilitary.about.com/od/ armytrng/a/sniperschool.htm; see also the U.S. Army Sniper Training Manual.

6. Yassin Musharbash, "What al-Qaida Really Wants," *Spiegel Online,* August 12, 2005.

7. Global Terror Alert, August 15, 2005, available at http://www.globalterror alert.com/pdf/0805/zarqawi-propaganda.pdf.

8. "Neither 'Stingy' nor Unpopular," *Wall Street Journal,* March 16, 2006.

9. Toby Harnden, "Three Iranian Factories Mass-Produce Bombs to Kill British in Iraq," *Sunday Telegraph,* August 20, 2006.

CHAPTER 6: ARE WE PREPARED?

1. Written Testimony of Mr. Max Mayfield, Director of the Tropical Prediction Center/National Hurricane Center, Before the Senate Committee on Commerce, Science, and Transportation Subcommittee on Disaster Prevention and Prediction, September 20, 2005, available at http://www. legislative.noaa.gov/Testimony/mayfieldfinal092005.pdf#search=%22%22 Max%20Mayfield%22%20%22September%2020%2C%202005% 22%22.

2. National Weather Service Issues Special Hurricane Warning 4 PM CDT, August 28, 2005.

3. "Hurricane Camille—August 17–18, 1969," Maritime & Seafood Industry Museum, available at http://www.maritimemuseum.org/camille/.

4. "Washing Away," *New Orleans Times-Picayune,* June 23–27, 2002.

5. Senate Homeland Security and Governmental Affairs, Hearing on the Leadership Roles of DHS and FEMA in Response to Hurricane Katrina, February 10, 2006.

6. A more detailed discussion of the innovations that have taken place in New York can be found at http://www.security.state.ny.us/.

7. Dr. James Jay Carafano, "The Senate's Katrina Report Draft: Hits and Misses," The Heritage Foundation, April 27, 2006.

CHAPTER 7: WHAT YOU DON'T KNOW ABOUT OUR BORDERS

1. Donald L. Barlett and James B. Steele, "Who Left the Door Open?" *Time,* March 30, 2006.

2. Demetrios Papademetriou, co-director of the International Migration Policy Program at the Carnegie Endowment for International Peace, testimony before the Subcommittee on Immigration and Claims of the Committee on the Judiciary, U.S. House of Representatives, April 14, 1999, available at http://www.carnegieendowment.org/publications/ index.cfm?fa=view&id=224.

3. "Ahmed Ressam's Millennium Plot," PBS *Frontline,* available at http:// www.pbs.org/wgbh/pages/frontline/shows/trail/inside/cron.html.

4. Ibid.

5. Jerry Seper, "Border Patrol Told to Stand Down in Arizona," *Washington Times,* May 13, 2005.

6. Ibid.

7. CBS *Evening News,* July 9, 2006; NBC *Nightly News,* July 9, 2006.

8. "U.S. Ending 'Catch and Release' at Mexico Border," Reuters, November 23, 2005, available at http://www.msnbc.msn.com/id/10173883/from/RL.1.

9. Spencer S. Hsu, "Immigration Arrests Down 8% for Year," *Washington Post,* October 31, 2006; Michael Hedges, "Official: Border Arrests Dropping," *Houston Chronicle,* October 30, 2006.

10. Congressional Research Service, "9/11 Commission: Current Legislation Proposals for U.S. Immigration Law and Policy," October 18, 2004.

11. Janice L. Kephart, "Immigration and Terrorism: Moving Beyond the 9/11 Staff Report on Terrorist Travel," Center for Immigration Studies, September 2005.

12. Stephen Dinan, "Agency Faulted for Visa Overstays," *Washington Times,* June 3, 2004, available at http://www.washingtontimes.com/national/20040603-112812-1736r.htm.

13. Adrian Sainz, "INS Visas Arrive for Two 9/11 Hijackers," Associated Press, March 13, 2002.

14. Patty Croom and Kathy Bellows, "Understanding the Student and Exchange Visitor Information System," *EDUCAUSE Quarterly,* 2002.

15. Carl Levin, "Security of Ocean Shipping Containers," May 26, 2005.

16. "Forrester Recommends Corrective-Action Program to Protect Freight Transportation," *Manufacturing Business Technology,* January 1, 2005.

17. Ibid.

18. "Singapore, the World's Busiest Seaport, Implements the Container Security Initiative and Begins to Target and Pre-Screen Cargo Destined for U.S.," U.S. Department of Homeland Security, U.S. Customs and Border Protection, March 17, 2003.

19. Stephen E. Flynn and Lawrence M. Wein, "Think Inside the Box," *New York Times,* November 29, 2005.

20. Jay Etta Z. Hecks, Director of Physical Infrastructure Issues, Testimony Before the House Committee on Government Reform Subcommittee on National Security, Veterans Affairs, and International Relations, August 5, 2002.

21. Stephen E. Flynn, "Port Security Is Still a House of Cards," *Far Eastern*

Economic Review, January/February 2006, available at http://www.feer. com/articles1/2006/0601/free/p005.html.

CHAPTER 8: BRAVEST OF THE BRAVE, LED BY IDIOTS

1. Drew Brown, "Illness Takes Greater Toll than Combat," Knight Ridder Newspapers, October 29, 2006.
2. Anita Manning, "Skin Lesions Afflict Troops," *USA Today,* December 5, 2003.
3. "Vaccines Eyed in GI's Death," CBS News, November 19, 2003; "Mandatory Anthrax Shots Stir Health Fears, Sap Morale," *USA Today,* December 12, 2003; "Anthrax Vaccinations Halted Again," United Press International, October 28, 2004; Jeff Schogol, "Group Fighting Mandatory Anthrax Vaccinations." *Stars and Stripes,* October 29, 2006.
4. Eric Boehlert, "A Shot in the Dark," *Salon,* December 10, 2003, available at http://dir.salon.com/story/news/feature/2003/12/10/anthrax/index _np.html.
5. Mark Benjamin, "Sick, Wounded U.S. Troops Held in Squalor," UPI, October 17, 2003; Frederick Sweet, "Maimed in Iraq, Then Mistreated, Neglected, and Hidden in America," *Christian Science Monitor,* July 7, 2003.
6. Brown, "Illness Takes Greater Toll than Combat."
7. John Althouse, "Army Chief: Force to Occupy Iraq Massive," *USA Today,* February 25, 2003.
8. Press Briefing on Overview of Operation Restoring Rights in Tall Afar, Iraq, Presenter: Army Col. H. R. McMaster, commander of the 3rd Armored Cavalry Regiment, U.S. Department of Defense Office of the Assistant Secretary of Defense (Public Affairs).
9. *Talk of the Nation,* NPR, April 25, 2006.
10. "Editorial: A Failure of Leadership at the Highest Levels," *Army Times,* May 17, 2004.
11. Michael Duffy, "The Shame of Kilo Company," *Time,* June 5, 2006.

CHAPTER 9: HANDS OFF

1. *Congressional Record,* October 25, 2001.
2. Judge Andrew P. Napolitano, *The Constitution in Exile* (Nashville: Nelson Current, 2006), p. 222.

3. Barton Gellman, "The FBI's Secret Scrutiny: In Hunt for Terrorists, Bureau Examines Records of Ordinary Americans," *Washington Post,* November 6, 2005.

4. Dan Eggen, "Key Part of Patriot Act Ruled Unconstitutional: Internet Providers' Data at Issue," *Washington Post,* September 30, 2004; Declan McCullagh, "Judge Disarms Patriot Act Proviso," CNETNews.com, September 29, 2004.

5. Letter from Senator Jay Rockefeller to Vice President Dick Cheney, July 17, 2003, available at http://www.fas.org/irp/news/2005/12/rock121 905.pdf.

6. For a detailed explanation of the unit's tasks, see: Prepared statement of Anthony A Shaffer, Lieutenant Colonel, U.S. Army Reserve, Senior Intelligence Officer, before the House Armed Services Committee, Congress of the United States, February 15, 2006.

7. United States Citizen and Immigration Service Services, Naturalization Oath of Allegiance to the United States of America.

8. "Person of the Week: Jose Padilla," *Time,* June 24, 2006.

9. Robert Young Pelton, "Inside the Afghan War Machine," *National Geographic Adventure Magazine,* March 2002.

CHAPTER 10: WHAT WE CAN DO?

1. "Troops Put Thorny Questions to Rumsfeld," CNN.com, December 9, 2004, available at http://www.cnn.com/2004/WORLD/meast/12/08/rumsfeld. troops/.

2. Kelly M. Greenhill, "Don't Dumb Down the Army," *New York Times,* February 17, 2006.

3. Fran Spielman, "Daley: By 2016, Cameras on 'Almost Every Block,' " *Chicago Sun-Times,* October 12, 2006.

4. Michael Goldfarb, "Improvised Explosive Disaster: An Inside Look at the Pentagon's Inadequate Response to the IED Threat in Iraq," *Weekly Standard,* May 3, 2006.

5. Budget of the United States Government, Fiscal Year 2007, Office of Management and Budget.

6. "Soldiers with Traumatic Brain Injury (TBI)," Brain Injury Association of America, February 2005, available at http://www.biausa.org/word.files. to.pdf/good.pdfs/advocacyweek2005/soldierswithTBI8.pdf.

7. See http://www.operation-helmet.org/.

8. Vik Jolly, "Marines to Get Helmet Pads: Pendleton's Marine's Grandfather Tried for Years to Convince the Corps of Benefits," *Orange County Register*, October 11, 2006.

9. James Bamford, "The Man Who Sold the War," *Rolling Stone*, November 17, 2005.

ACKNOWLEDGMENTS

This book would not have been possible without the efforts of many. Thanks to Roger Ailes and the people at Fox News who give me a platform to talk about the things that are important to me; to Mr. Bill O'Reilly for your friendship and encouragement; Mr. Eric Simonoff for convincing a publisher to take another chance on me; and to Jed Donahue and the dedicated staff at Crown Forum.

Christine Hunsinger and Kathie Hackett spent their valuable time reviewing and correcting my many mistakes; because they did, this book is better.

As always, my family's, especially my wife, Angela's, encouragement and faith in me has made all the difference. Thanks, guys.

INDEX